CAD Modeling Essentials in 3DEXPERIENCE 2016x Using CATIA Applications

Nader G. Zamani
University of Windsor

SDC
Publications

SDC Publications
P.O. Box 1334
Mission, KS 66222
913-262-2664
www.SDCpublications.com
Publisher: Stephen Schroff

ISBN-13: 978-1-63057-095-8
ISBN-10: 1-63057-095-8

Printed and bound in the United States of America.

Dedicated to

Zidan N., Jahan S., and Veda A.

Preface

This book has a tutorial style format and is written for those who want to learn the CAD basics in the 3DEXPERIENCE software by Dassault Systèmes. There is no secret that the best way to learn and master a software is by personal exploration which is strictly curiosity driven. Needless to say, although this may be the best strategy, it is extremely inefficient and perhaps very frustrating.

The purpose of this book is to present the reader with the essential threads on different basic topics dealing with CAD and let him/her to make further exploration. Since the 3DEXPERIENCE software has only recently been introduced, there are very few practical references and publications available in the public domain. In fact, at the time of the publication (2017), the present book is the only one available in this category. For those who may also be interested in more in-depth applications of 3DEXPERIENCE in solving practical engineering problems, there are two other tutorial style textbooks by the same author and publisher. These more advanced books are dealing with the applications of 3DEXPERIENCE in Finite Element Analysis and the Mechanism Design modeling.

I sincerely hope that you enjoy this book and find it useful in your future academic endeavours.

Nader Zamani
Windsor, Ontario

TABLE OF CONTENTS

Introduction
and the Basic Settings

Preamble:

Early in 2012, the Dassault Systemes (DS) Corporation introduced the 3DEXPERIENCE business platform as their major product, with the strategic goal of integrating a large number of applications in this platform. Among the applications of interest to the readers of this book are Catia, SOLIDWORKS, Enovia, and Simulia. It is just about impossible, and perhaps meaningless, to expect a typical user to be interested in and familiar with all the applications available in 3DEXPERIENCE.

Although the software mentioned above will be available on a stand-alone basis for a few more years, in the near future they will be considered as legacy software and their "ghost" can be accessed only via the 3DEXPERIENCE platform. At this point in time, the DS strategy is to provide the academic licenses of the 3DEXPERIENCE not on "premise" but on the "cloud" basis. Although this will eliminate the software administration and update issues from the academia's point of view, server access on demand (24/7) by students is a challenge that needs to be addressed by DS. Another major shift by DS is the abandoning of the standard file structure (type/location) in favor of strictly database structure. It is worth mentioning that for the non-academic clients, a private "cloud" option is also available. In all likelihood, this is the preferred method of "cloud" access by industrial clients.

As time progresses, the number and quality of the teaching/training resources in 3DEXPERIENCE will grow on the web, but at this point, there are fairly limited resources available to students. Needless to say, major DS clients can afford arranging training sessions offered by the DS professionals and resellers at any cost. This is not a luxury available to a typical private individual/student. The purpose of the present tutorial book is to introduce the reader to the bare essentials of the platform in the context of CAD functionalities. It is by no means intended to be a comprehensive and/or completely organized approach to all the available features. The goal is to merely show the "ropes" and leave further exploration to the reader.

The readers who have previous exposure (experience) to Catia v5, fortunately or unfortunately, have an advantage over others. Many of the features in the CAD applications have been directly incorporated in 3DEXPERIENCE. This is particularly true in the case of Part Design and the Generative Shape Design currently available in Catia v5. There have been significant changes in the Assembly Design application. If you are a first time user with no previous experience in v5, there is no reason to despair as the tutorial approach of this book will provide the necessary skills. Upon the completion of this elementary book, the reader can find more advanced applications in the complementary textbooks by the author listed below.

1- Finite Element Essentials in 3DEXPERIENCE, by Nader G. Zamani, SDC Publications, 2017.

2- Mechanism Design Essentials in 3DEXPERIENCE, by Nader G. Zamani, SDC Publications, 2017.

Dashboard Interface:

Upon receiving permission to use the
3DEXPERIENCE on the cloud, you will receive a
communication from DS to be able to register on
their website and set your password. This is
commonly referred to your "3D Passport Login."
In your "login" session to the system, you are
prompted to enter password as shown on the right.

After a successful login, the interface below, which is referred to as your "Dashboard,"
will appear. This dashboard is fully customizable but the details/experimenting with
customization are left to the reader as it is not relevant to the beginners.

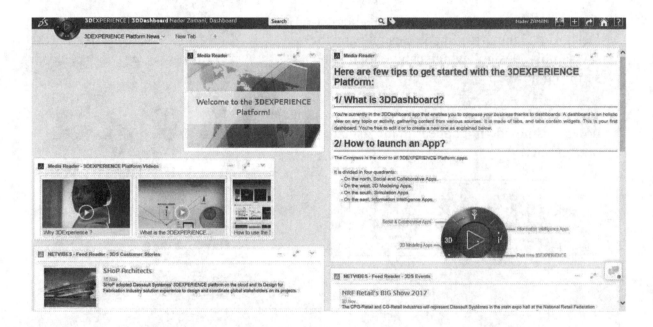

The radio dial shown on the right is of great
significance in 3DEXPERIENCE and is referred to as
the "Compass" by DS. The compass is divided into
four sectors: North, South, East, and West. They each
deal with a particular aspect of the platform
summarized below.

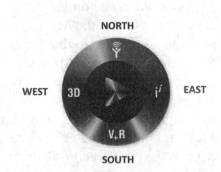

NORTH:	Social and Collaborative Apps.
EAST:	Information Intelligence Apps.
SOUTH:	Content and Simulation Apps.
WEST:	3D Modeling Apps. (This is the sector relevant to the present book)

Accessing your 3D Modeling Apps:

In this book, you are primarily working in the WEST sector of the compass. Click the WEST sector, as shown on the right.

Left click on the WEST sector of the compass on the top left corner of your dashboard.

The menu shown on the right is being displayed. The list of all the Modeling Apps (in the form of icons) appears as shown.

The most common Apps used in this book are "Part Design," "Generative Shape Design" and the "Assembly Design" which can be found upon scrolling down.

The icons are displayed below for your perusal; however, they do not appear in the list adjacent to one another.

It is possible to customize your dashboard view with "My Favorite Apps" bar so that the most commonly used Apps are grouped together. For the author, this is shown on the right. Although the organizing may take a few minutes and some trial and error, it is very valuable as there will be no need to search through the large number of icons available.

Author's frequently used Applications (App.)

From the list, select the "Part Design App." After a brief pause the compass shown on the right appears again, which is an indication that the App has started.

The dialogue box below opens next which shows the default identifier for the 3DEXPERIENCE file associated with the 3D part. In this case, the label "Physical Product00027679" is automatically generated. The label (name) can be changed at this point; however, there is a more efficient way of handling such customization. The process is described next.

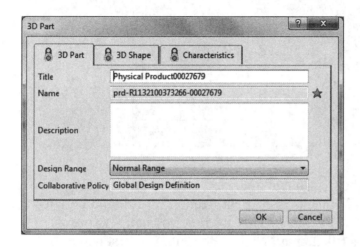

From the top right corner of the screen, shown below, select the "Me" icon followed by "Preferences." This results in the "Preferences" dialogue box opening, shown on the next page. The Catia v5 users may recognize this as the "Options" dialogue box where all the settings were accessible.

This has exactly the same functionalities. Any desired deviations from the default settings in 3DEXPERIENCE have to be initiated through this window.

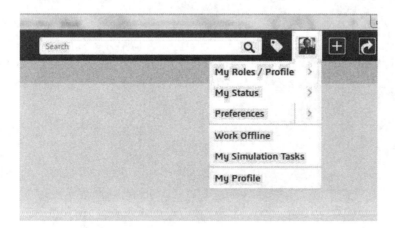

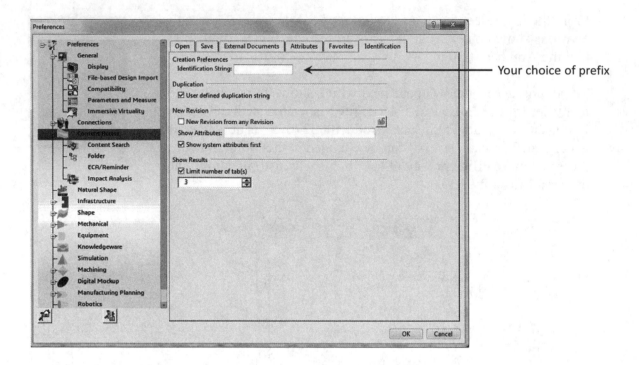

Your choice of prefix

Using the cursor, navigate through the tree shown in the left column of the dialogue box until you are at the "Connect Access" branch. The "Identification" tab should be selected. Note that the "Identification String" box is blank. This is where you can set your "desired" prefix. For example, it was filled in as "Nader," the author's first name as shown below. By doing this, all "automatic" identifiers are prefixed with "Nader." A prefix greatly simplifies a search in the "cloud" database.

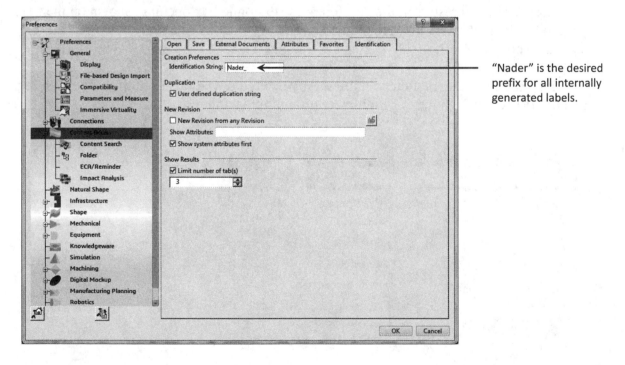

"Nader" is the desired prefix for all internally generated labels.

To ensure that the process has in fact worked, try creating another 3D part. Repeat the steps starting on top of page 1-4. This time, the prefix "Nader" is added to the label.

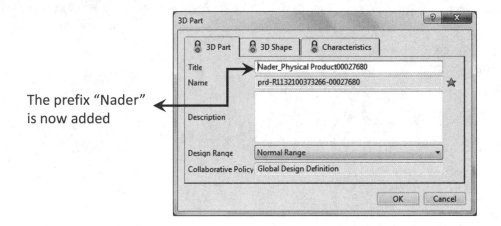

The prefix "Nader" is now added

Upon accepting this information by clicking on "OK," the new 3D part and the associated tree structure appears on the screen as shown below. Note that there are two tabs on the screen. The "Physical Product00027679" tab, which is grey, is the original one created. The white active tab, the "Nader_Physical Product00027680," is the second one created where the prefix "Nader" was employed.

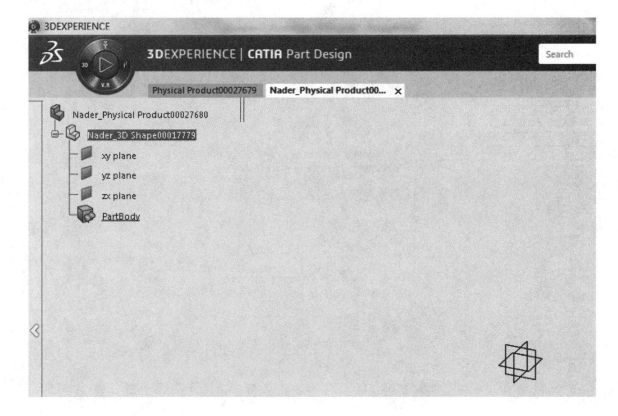

Since there is no need to keep the first file, one can close it. First select the inactive tab and click on "X" to close it. This is shown on the right.

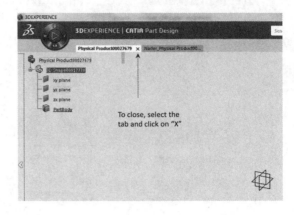

You are then prompted as shown below to acknowledge that the part has not been saved. Click on "No."

To close, select the tab and click on "X"

At this point, only "Nader_Physical Product00027680" stays on your screen. Before doing any further work, you will be saving this item.

Click the icon [⤴] from the top right corner of the screen and choose "Save."

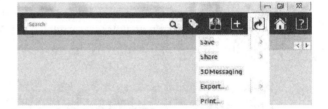

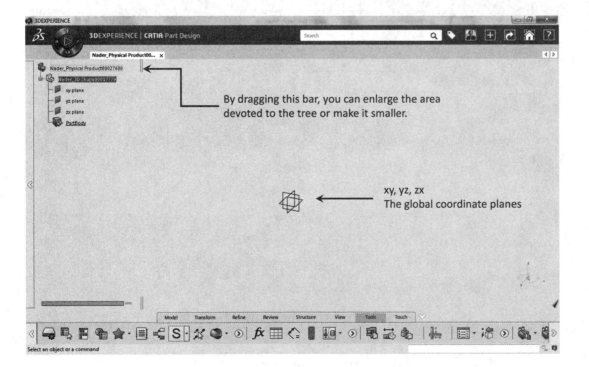

By dragging this bar, you can enlarge the area devoted to the tree or make it smaller.

xy, yz, zx
The global coordinate planes

Setting the Units:

In order to specify the units in 3DEXPERIENCE, you need to access the "Preferences" dialogue box. The steps to access this window were explained in the middle of page 1-5. Please refer to the appropriate page. When the dialogue box is accessed, as shown on the right, navigate through the tree to select the branch "Parameters and Units."

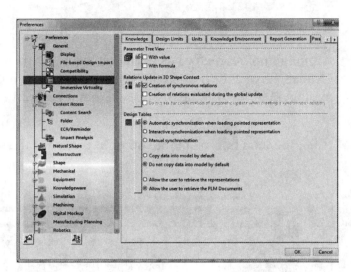

Select the "Units" tab from the top right side of the dialogue box. Choose the appropriate variable (for example, length as shown). Finally, with the pulldown menu, select the desired unit. In the figure below, "mm" is chosen.

It is worth mentioning that in doing so, "mm" is the default unit but during the modeling process, you can input the length in any units, such as "m," "cm," "in," etc., as long as they are specified. The inputted (typed) values are then automatically converted into mm. For example, at any point, if you type "1in," it is internally converted and displayed as "25.4mm."

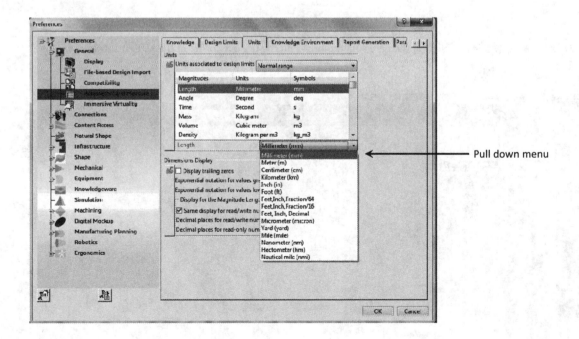

Pull down menu

Saving and Retrieving Data from the Cloud:

Although no geometry has been created so far, it is worth trying to save the "Nader_Physical Product00027680" data and trying to retrieve it. The steps for save were explained in the middle of page 1-8 but repeated here.

Click the icon ![icon] from the top right corner of the screen and choose "Save."

A pop-up box indicates that the data is being saved remotely on the DS server.

You will now exit the Part Design App by clicking on the compass located on the top right corner of the screen and selecting "Close" as shown below.

To Exit the 3D Modeling, click on the very small compass on the top left corner of the screen and select "Close"

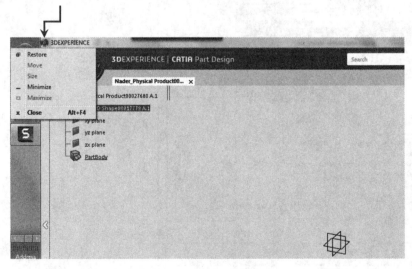

Return to your dashboard. In the search area of the dashboard, type "Nader_Physical Product00027680" and hit return as shown below.

In the search box of your dashboard type "Nader_Physical Product00027680"

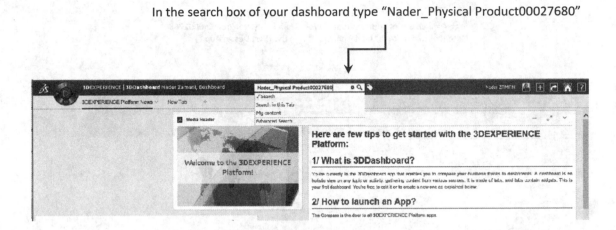

The file is then located within the "cloud" and ready to be retrieved.

By double clicking on the located file, detailed information can be displayed; however, the file cannot be opened while in the dashboard.

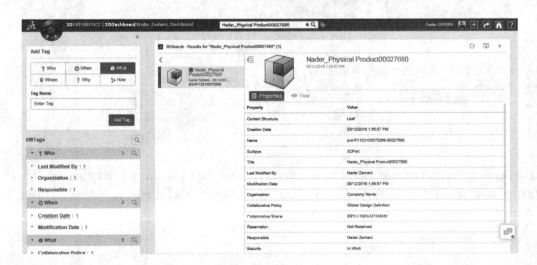

Select the "WEST" sector of the compass in the top left corner of the screen, followed by the Part Design App in the list as shown below. Note that this view is not in the dashboard but it is in the Part Design App.

In the search box of your dashboard type "Nader_Physical Product00027680"
Note that this is not in the dashboard, it is in the "Part Design App."

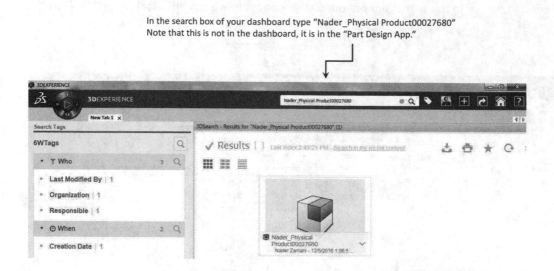

Upon completing the above step, the following screen pops up.

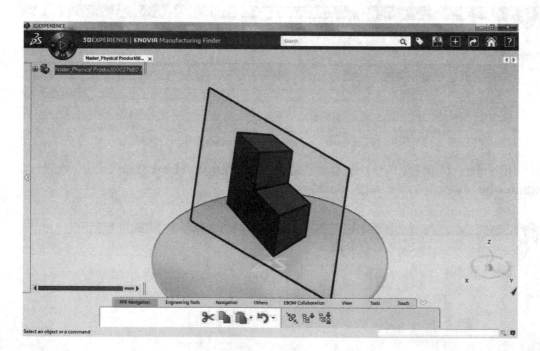

You are now in a position to open the file and retrieve the material already saved. This can easily be achieved by double clicking on the top branch of the tree. Namely, double clicking of "Nader_Physical Product00027680."

This can also be achieved by placing the cursor on the top branch and right clicking. Select "Open" from the contextual menu as shown below.

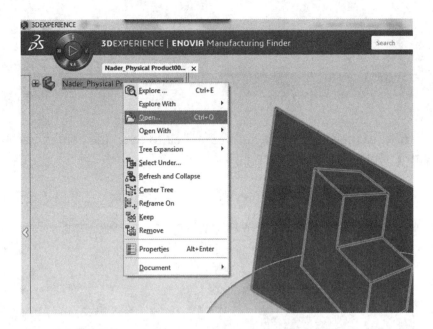

The end result of both approaches explained above is the same. The file "Nader_Physical Product00027680" opens as shown below. Needless to say, this file currently has no geometry in it. Not surprisingly, your screen appears as shown below.

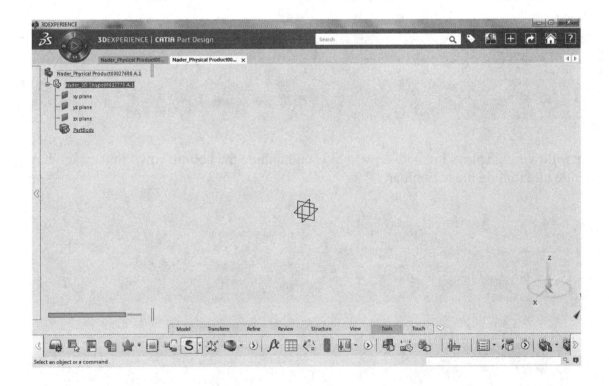

In the event that the bottom set of icons on your screen appears as in the view below, you can customize it to look like the figure on the previous page. The bottom row of icons is also referred to as the **"Action Bar."**

Place the cursor on the row next to the description, and right click to open the contextual menu. Select "Sections with Labels."

Place curser in this row, right click for the contextual menu to open. Select "Sections with Labels"

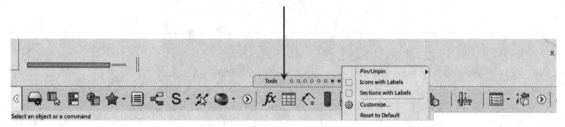

The above steps change the bottom row of icons as shown below. This arrangement is more useful than the one above and it is much easier to navigate with.

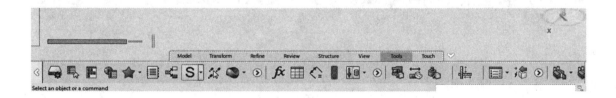

The following displays indicate how to hide and unhide the bottom row toolbar (i.e., how to hide and unhide the action bar.)

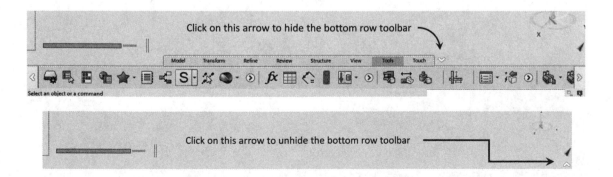

Click on this arrow to hide the bottom row toolbar

Click on this arrow to unhide the bottom row toolbar

In order to sign out of the dashboard, select "Me" from the top right corner of the screen and once the contextual menu appears, select "Sign Out."

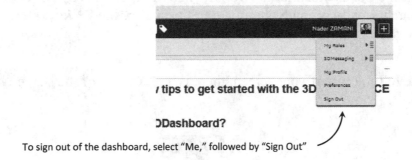

To sign out of the dashboard, select "Me," followed by "Sign Out"

Tree Essentials:

The familiarity with the tree is essential for working in 3DEXPERIENCE. If the tree disappears, either intentionally or inadvertently, don't panic; try the **F3 key**. Depressing this key hides and unhides the tree.

Furthermore, on the left margin of your screen, there is an "Arrow" of the shape ◀. See the figure below.

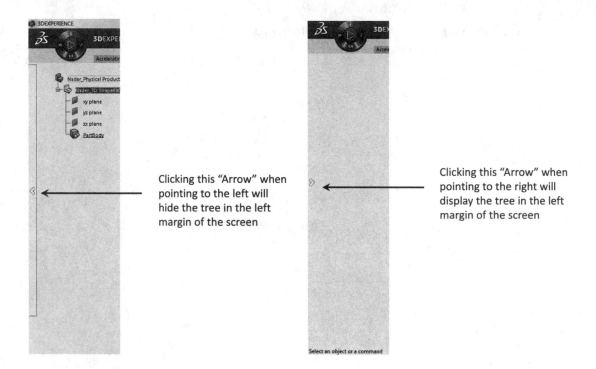

Clicking this "Arrow" when pointing to the left will hide the tree in the left margin of the screen

Clicking this "Arrow" when pointing to the right will display the tree in the left margin of the screen

A more controlled approach for showing or hiding the tree is by right clicking of the mouse on the screen. From the "Display" menu, make sure the "Tree Display" is checked.

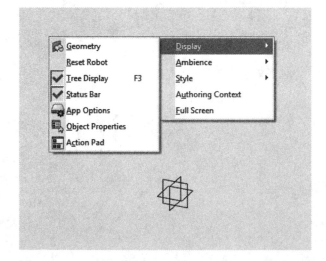

Warning:
During work with the software, if your geometry disappears and you have no idea why it happened, your first approach should be to select the "Geometry" from the display menu shown on the right. If this action has no effect, you should look into it deeper.

For the sake of completeness, the effect of selecting "Ambience" and "Style" is also shown below.

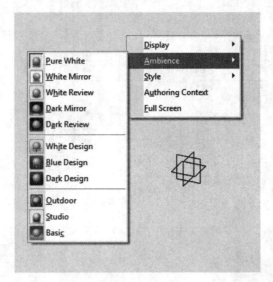

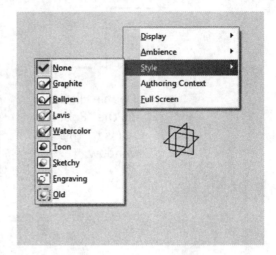

Clicking on this black

"Arrow" 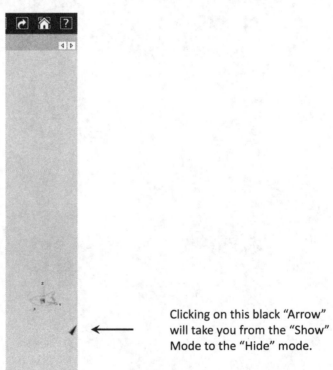 in the bottom, right margin of the screen will take you from the "Show" mode to the "Hide" mode. Any geometric object in 3DEXPERIENCE that is hidden is placed in the "Hide" mode which can be accessed via the mentioned black arrow

Clicking on this black "Arrow" will take you from the "Show" Mode to the "Hide" mode.

The coordinate system shown in the bottom right margin of the screen is referred to as the "Robot." In Catia v5, this was referred to as "Compass."
Double clicking on the robot leads to a dialogue box which facilitates the precise positioning of the "Robot" when dealing with CAD modeling.

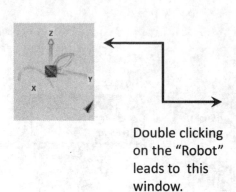

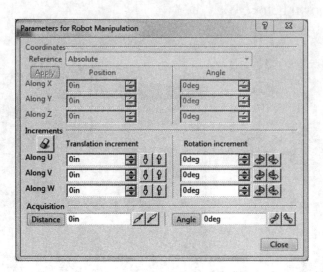

Double clicking
on the "Robot"
leads to this
window.

Making a Hammer

Objective:

In this chapter, you will explore the process of making a simple hammer as shown in the figure below. These are nominal dimensions in (mm) and only certain basic icons will be used in this problem. After making the hammer, some other features of the Part Design App will be explored which are not reflected in the drawing. In order to create the model, including accessing the App, setting up your units, and naming conventions, you need to follow the instructions in chapter 1.

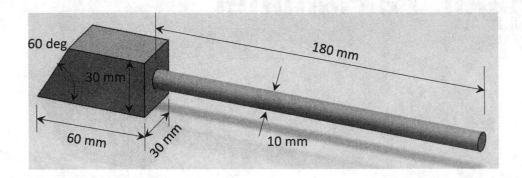

Enter the Part Design App 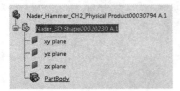 and create a part with the name of your choice. Here, the name below was used.

Nader_Hammer_CH2_Physical Product00030794

1- Select the yz plane from the tree or the screen and choose the "Position Sketched" icon 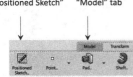 from the bottom row menu (i.e., from the action bar). Note that the "Positioned Sketch" is in the "Model" tab. This will land you in the Sketcher App.

•

2- Select the "Rectangle" icon  from the bottom row (i.e., the action bar) and draw a rectangle in an arbitrary location. Note that the "Rectangle" icon belongs to a submenu with many other choices shown on the right.

Obviously there are other ways of making a rectangle.

The tree shows you that rectangle has been created in "Sketch.1." Also, note that there is a background grid with default spacing.

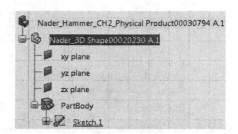

Before setting the dimensions of the hammer in the sketcher, a few words about the background grid is in order.

The grid spacing and the "graduation" of the grid can be changed by following the steps given next. Select the "Me" icon from the right top corner of the screen and click on "Preferences."

This leads to the following window.

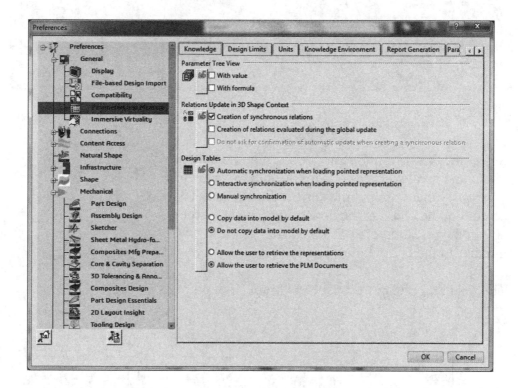

Choose the "Mechanical" branch followed by "Sketcher." This is where these parameters are set. The current values are 100mm and a graduation of 10 (see the top of the next page). The changing of the units was already discussed in chapter 1 (page 9).

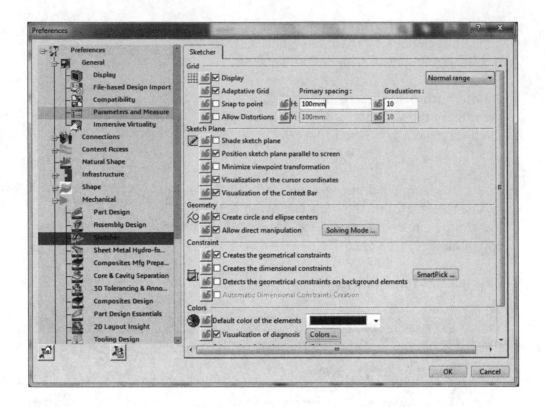

3- Select the "Constraint" icon 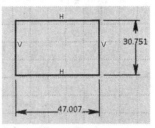 from the bottom menu and create dimensions for the sides as shown. Obviously these are not the correct dimensions. To do so, double click on the dimension (one at a time) and in the resulting dialogue box, change the number to the correct dimensions.

The resulting rectangle must be 60mm x 30mm.

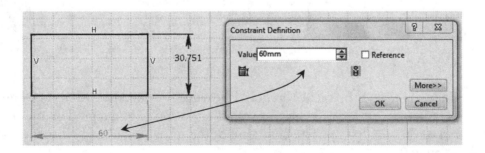

4- Next, using the "Line" icon 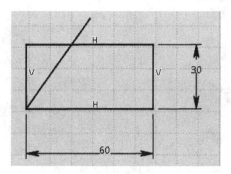 draw a slanted line from the bottom left corner in an arbitrary orientation.

Select the "Constraint" icon 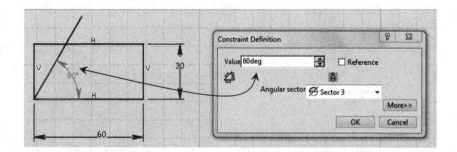 from the bottom menu and create angular dimensions between the slanted line and the horizontal base of the rectangle. To create an angle dimension, after selecting the icon use the cursor to select the two lines involved. Do not panic if the color of the dimensions begin to change after selecting the first line.

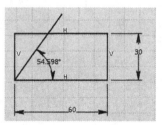

To change the dimension to 60 degrees, double click on the dimension and change it in the resulting dialogue box.

5- The next step is to trim the rectangle with the line. There are different ways of doing this but it is recommended to use the

"Quick Trim" 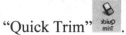 .

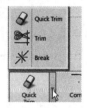

Note: Since you have to use the "Quick Trim" icon repeatedly (three times), it is better if you double clicked on it, which keeps it active until you select a different icon.

With the "Quick Trim" icon selected, follow the three steps shown below.

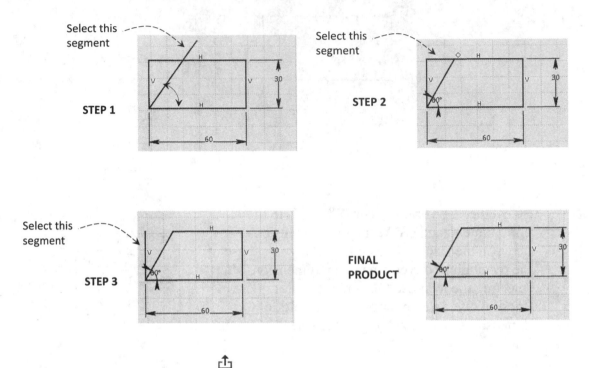

6- Use the "Exit App" icon to exit the sketcher and land in the 3D space. This App is one of the icons in the bottom row of icons (i.e., in the action bar).

7- Select the "Pad" icon from the action bar to open the "Pad" dialogue box. For the "Selection" pick "Sketch.1" from the screen or from the tree. For "Length," input 30 mm.

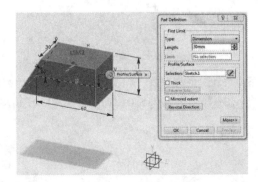

8- Once the pad is completed, select the face of the hammer as shown and pick the

"Positioned Sketch" icon 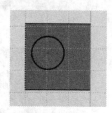 . You will be drawing a circle of diameter 10 mm on this face.

Using the "Circle" icon 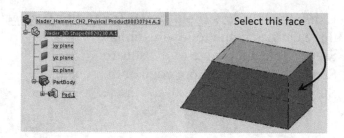 draw a circle.

Notice that the center of the circle is not symmetrically positioned within the square face selected. Of course, this can easily be corrected by imposing dimensional constraints between the center and the edges. However, you are shown an alternative way to achieve this.

Using the Ctrl key (**held down for multiple selection**), select three entities in the following order:
Step 1: select left edge of the square.
Step 2: select the right edge of the square.
Step 3: select the center of the circle.

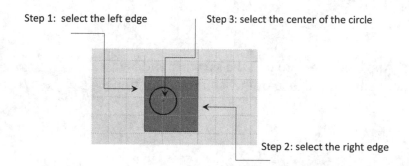

Click on the "Constraint…" icon 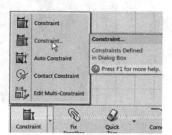 from the available choices shown on the right.

Upon completing the three steps and the selection of the above icon, a dialogue box appears.

Within this window, check the box labeled "Equidistant point." This will center the circle horizontally. Repeat the same process for the top edge, the bottom edge, and the center of the circle.

Using the Ctrl key (**held down for multiple selection**), select three entities in the following order:
Step 1: select top edge of the square.
Step 2: select the bottom edge of the square.
Step 3: select the center of the circle.

Once again, select the "Constraint..." icon 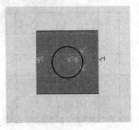 and check the "Equidistant point" option. The circle is now completely centered with the side face of the hammer regardless of the dimensions of the hammer. The design intent was to have a centered circle and this accomplished the task.

You now need to specify the diameter of the circle. Select the circle followed by the "Constraint" icon

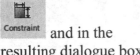 and in the resulting dialogue box enter 10 mm.

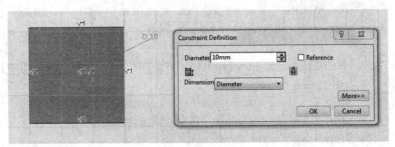

Use the "Exit App" icon 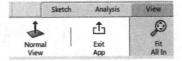 to exit the sketcher and land in the 3D space. This App is one of the icons in the action bar.

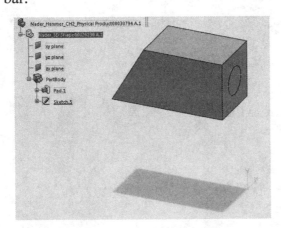

9- Select the circle just
created in the previous
step followed by the

"Pad" icon 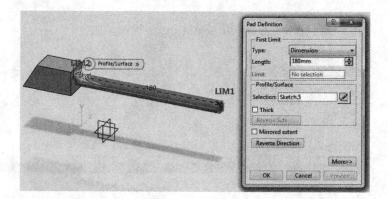. In the
resulting dialogue box
input 180 mm and close
the window.

Upon closing the "Pad Definition" window and checking the tree, you will notice two "Pad" features, Pad.1 which was the hammer head, and Pad.2 which is the hammer handle.

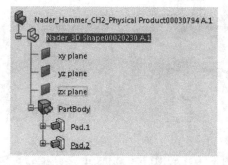

This completes the steps needed to create the hammer. The point discussed below is a very useful tool to change the dimensions of the geometry. The most straightforward approach to change a dimension (in the sketch) is to locate the appropriate sketch, and double click on the branch of the tree where the sketch resides. This will land you in the sketch where the appropriate changes can be made. An alternative approach is presented below.

Select the "Formula" icon *fx* Formula... from the "Tools" tab shown below.

Select the "Tools" tab

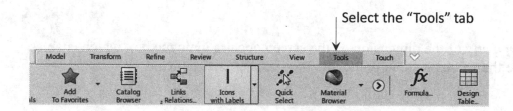

This leads to the following dialogue box.

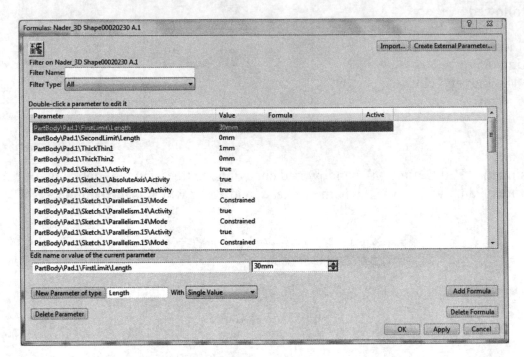

Selecting the Pad.1 from the tree (or with the cursor pointing to the hammer head) shows you the dimensions that were used to create the part as shown on the right.

Selecting the Pad.2 from the tree displays the dimensions of the hammer handle.

Double clicking any of the dimension on the screen opens a dialogue box which enables you to change the values without going into the sketcher environment.

Exercise 1:

Create the following solid object assuming that the supplied dimensions are in mm. In the event that some minor dimensions are missing estimate them based on the overall scale.

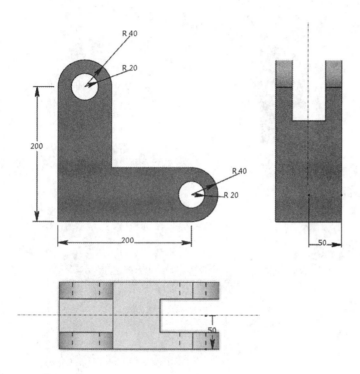

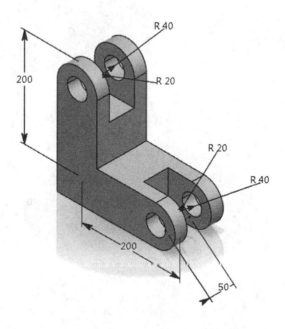

Exercise 2:

Create the following solid object assuming that the supplied dimensions are in mm. In the event that some minor dimensions are missing estimate them based on the overall scale.

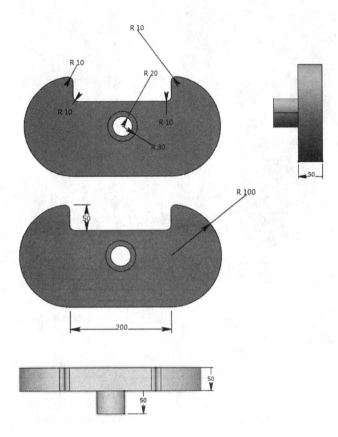

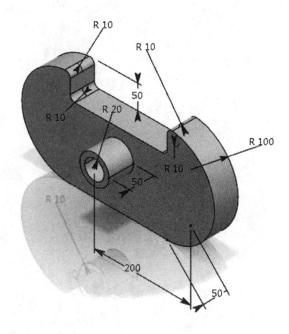

NOTES:

Chapter 03

Making a Connecting Rod

Objective:

In this chapter, you will explore the process of making a simple connecting rod as shown in the figure below. These are nominal dimensions in mm and only certain basic icons will be used in this problem. In order to create the model, including accessing the App, setting up your units, and naming conventions, you need to follow the instructions in chapter 1.

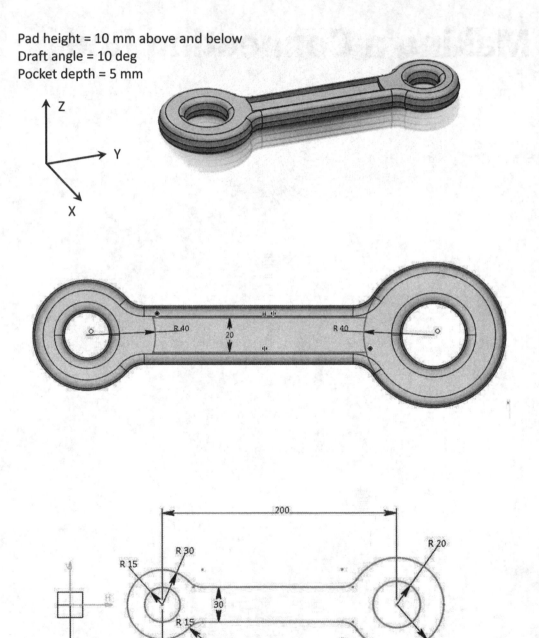

Pad height = 10 mm above and below
Draft angle = 10 deg
Pocket depth = 5 mm

Enter the Part Design App 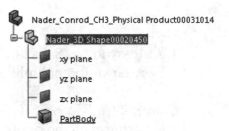 and create a part with the name of your choice. Here, the following name was used:

Nader_Conrod_CH3_Physical Product00030794

> Nader_Conrod_CH3_Physical Product00031014
> > Nader_3D Shape00020450
> > > xy plane
> > > yz plane
> > > zx plane
> > > PartBody

1- Select the xy plane from the tree or the screen and choose the "Positioned Sketch" icon from the bottom row menu (i.e., the action bar). Note that "Position Sketch" is in the "Model" tab. This will land you in the "Sketcher" application.

   In the event that your Sketcher grid is not showing, while in the sketcher, select the "Grid" icon.

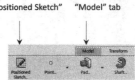

"Positioned Sketch"   "Model" tab

2- Choose the "Circle" icon from the bottom row and draw four circles in an arbitrary location; <u>**however, make sure that the centers of the circles are on the horizontal axis in the sketcher and that each pair is concentric.**</u>
Obviously there are other ways of making a circle.

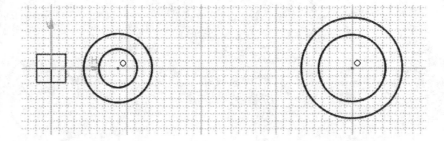

Note: Suppose that accidentally, two of the circles were drawn but are not concentric.

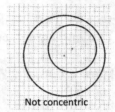
Not concentric

This is easy to fix. Select the two circles (use the Ctrl key down for multiple selection). Then use the

"Constraint...." icon 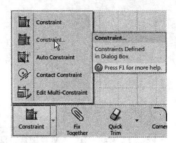 from the available choices shown on the right.

In the resulting dialogue box, check the "Concentric" option.

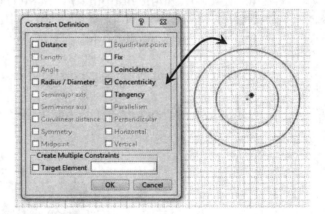

Select the "Constraint" icon 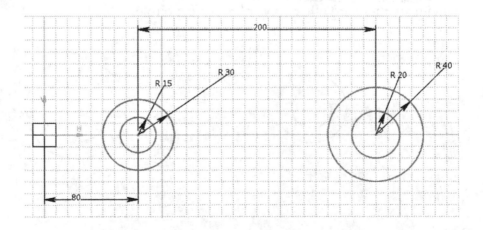 from the bottom row, and dimension to arrive at the following configuration.

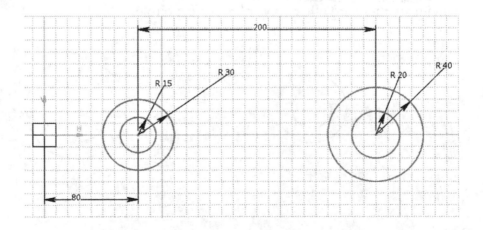

In order to have a better view of the sketcher, you can point the cursor to any dimensions, right click, and "Hide." This will clean up the screen.

Use the "Line" icon 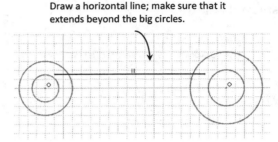 to draw a horizontal line above the center of circles and make sure that it extends beyond the two large circles. You will be using the "Quick Trim" icon to clean it up.

Draw a horizontal line; make sure that it extends beyond the big circles.

Selct the "Quick Trim" icon from the bottom row. With the cursor, select the end segments of the line beyond the large circles.

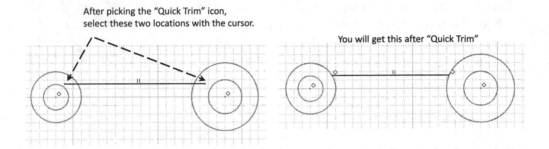

After picking the "Quick Trim" icon, select these two locations with the cursor.

You will get this after "Quick Trim"

Next, you will mirror the above line with respect to the horizontal axis in the sketcher. This was the reason that the circles had their centers on the horizontal axis.

Select the "Mirror" icon from the action bar.
Follow the instructions shown below. First select the line drawn and quick trimmed, followed by the horizontal axis in the sketcher plane. The result of mirroring is also shown below.

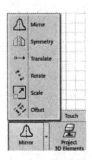

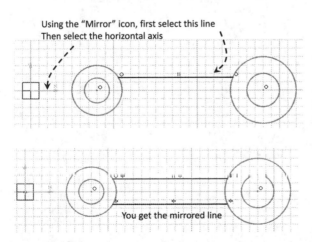

Using the "Mirror" icon, first select this line
Then select the horizontal axis

You get the mirrored line

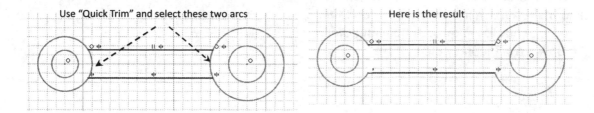

Once again, selct the "Quick Trim" icon to remove two arcs that are not needed as displayed below.

3- The next step is to create the fillets. Select the "Corner" icon **Corner** from the bottom row. Choose the corner point where the line joins the large circle (instead of picking the point, one may prefer to select the line and the arc of the circle). A fillet is created there.

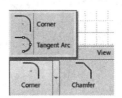

There are two ways to dimension the fillet. One approach is to use the "Constraint" icon **Constraint** to dimension it, and then change it. The second approach is to double click on the fillet arc to open the dialogue box shown below, and then change the radius to 15 mm as needed. The above process is repeated four times to get the four fillets needed.

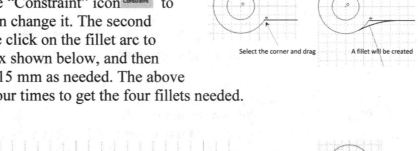

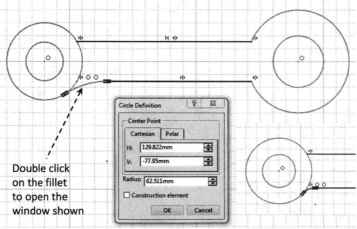

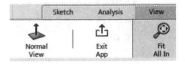

4- Use the "Exit App" icon to exit the sketcher and land in the 3D space. This App is one of the icons in the bottom row of icons (i.e., the action bar).

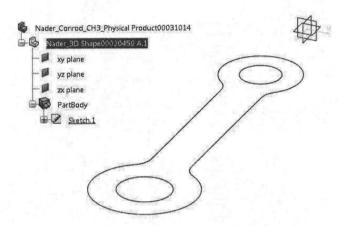

Select the "Drafted Filleted Pad" icon from the bottom row.

In the resulting dialogue box, input 10 mm for the "Length," 10 deg for the "Angle," and pick the xy-plane for "Second Limit." Finally, close the window by clicking on "OK."

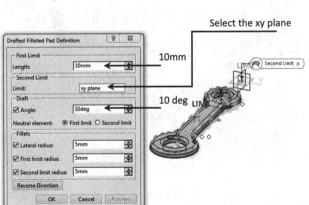

The result of this operation is shown on the right. This is not displayed with a good rendering. In the next page, the rendering styles are discussed.

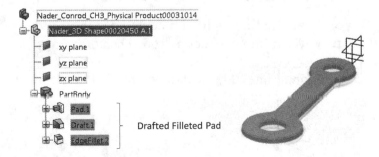

5- Select the "View"
tab from the bottom
row.

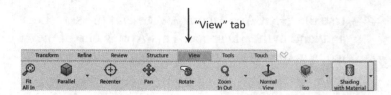

"View" tab

Then expand the menu which deals with
rendering styles. This is shown on the right. By
hovering the cursor over the different styles, you
can choose the one that best fits your needs. If

you select the "Shading with Edges" icon 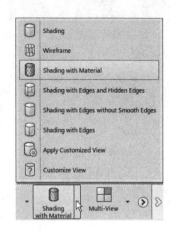,
the connecting rod (partially made) appears as
shown below.

Once again, select the
"Model" tab from the
bottom row to proceed
with the rest of the
construction.

"Model" tab

6- Select the top face of the part created and
enter the Sketcher. As a reminder, to achieve

this, select the "Positioned Sketch" icon
from the bottom row menu.
In the Sketcher, draw the two circular arcs

with radii R = 40 mm centered at the
two eyes of the connecting rod. Then draw a

Select this face,
enter Sketcher

horizontal line with a height of 10 mm above the local horizontal axis as shown
on the next page.

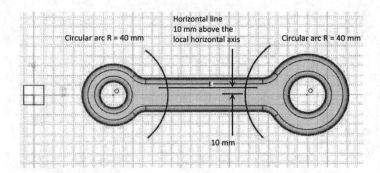

Note that the above dimensions are not set yet. Once these dimensions are specified, the drawing looks as shown on the right. The connecting rod has been hidden to maintain clarity (right click, Hide/Show 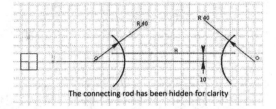).

Selct the "Quick Trim" icon 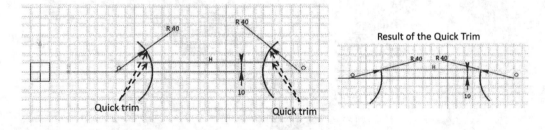 from the bottom row. With the cursor, select the end segments of the line beyond the large circles and the unwanted portions of the arcs.

Select the "Mirror" icon Mirror from the bottom row.
Follow the instruction shown on the right. First select the line drawn and quick trimmed, followed by the horizontal axis in the sketcher plane. The result of mirroring is also displayed.

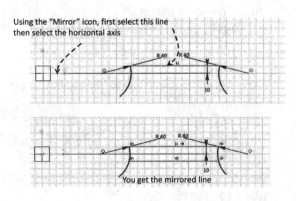

Once again, select the

"Quick Trim" icon 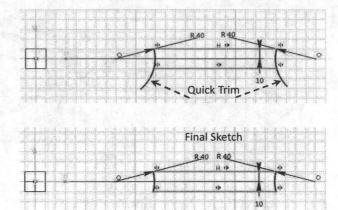 from the bottom row. Trim the unwanted portions of the arcs. The final result is shown on the right.

7- Use the "Exit App" icon 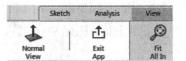 to exit the sketcher and land in the 3D space.

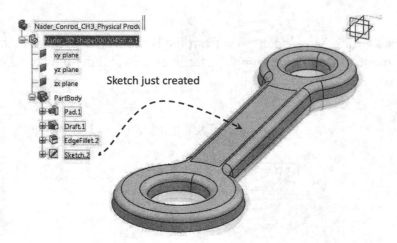

Sketch just created

Next, remove material of the given shape "Sketch.2" and a depth 5mm from the connecting rod. This is achieved by the "Pocketing" operation.

Select the "Pocket" icon 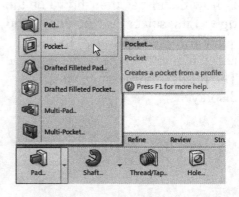 from the bottom row.

For the Profile Selection, select "Sketch.2" from the tree or the screen, and for the depth, input 5 mm. It is unlikely that you need to "Reverse Side."

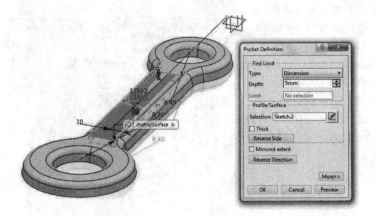

The pocket just created is shown below. Changes can be made by double clicking on the appropriate branch of the tree.

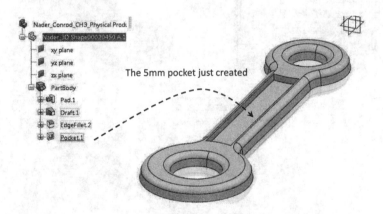

The 5mm pocket just created

8- The final step in the construction of the connecting rod is "Mirroring" of the geometry just created with respect to an appropriate plane. This operation is in the "Transform" tab of the bottom row of icons. Select the "Transform" tab.

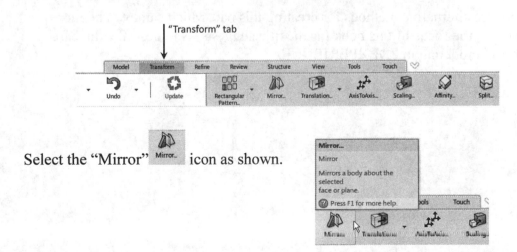

Select the "Mirror" ⬙ icon as shown.

The dialogue box "Mirror Definition" shown on the right pops up. For the "Mirroring element" which represents the symmetry plane, either xy plane or the bottom plane of the part created can be selected. The "Object to mirror" should be "Current Solid."

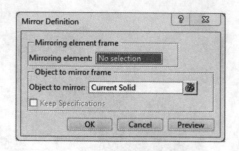

Once these two tasks are completed, the final CAD model of the connecting rod is displayed on your screen.

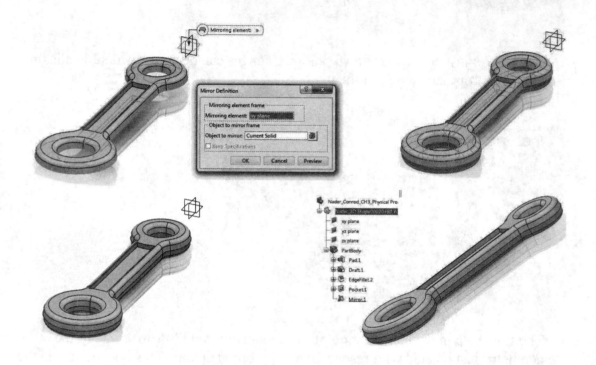

Obviously there are alternative methods for creating this part which can even be more efficient. However, the focus of this book (as the title suggests) is to describe the bare essentials of CAD modeling in 3DEXPERIENCE.

Exercise 1:

Create the following solid model. Use the dimensions shown where the units are in inches.

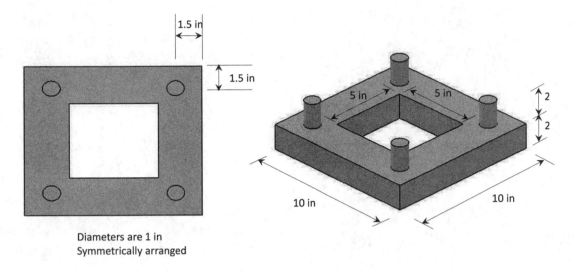

Diameters are 1 in
Symmetrically arranged

Exercise 2:

Create the following solid model. Use the dimensions shown where the units are in inches.

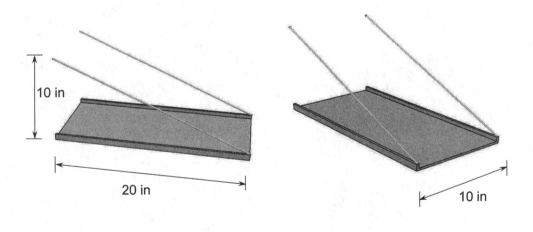

Front view (not to scale)

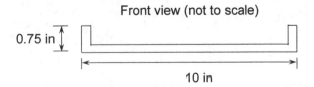

NOTES:

Applying Simple
Material Properties to a Part

Objective:

The main objective of this chapter is to demonstrate one approach to apply material properties to a part constructed with the Part Design App. The concept of "Circular Pattern" is also introduced along the way.

The part to be modelled is shown below where the dimensions are clearly specified. Needless to say, there are different ways to create the model. The approach in this chapter is one of such strategies.

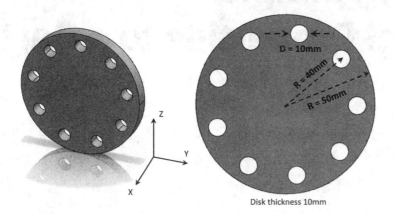

Disk thickness 10mm

Once the part is created, the following material properties are specified.

Young's Modulus = 200 GPa
Poisson's Ratio = 0.3
Mass Density = 1000 kg/m^3
Coefficient of Thermal Expansion = 10 µm/m-K
Coefficient of Thermal Conductivity = 50 W/m-K
Coefficient of Thermal Heat Capacity = 0.5 J/g-K

As the reader will see, all such coefficients can be temperature dependent and Excel can be uploaded to populate the material property section as a function temperature (tabular form). For the sake of simplicity, it is assumed that all such data are at the specific room temperature of 293K (Kelvin).

Creation of the Part:

Enter the Part Design App 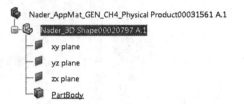 and create a part with the name of your choice. Here, the following name is used:

Nader_AppMat_CH4_Physical Product00030794

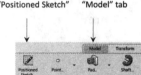

1- Select the zy plane from the tree or the screen and choose the "Positioned Sketch" icon ![Positioned Sketch] from the bottom row menu (i.e., the action bar). Note that the "Positioned Sketch" is in the "Model" tab. This will land you in the sketcher application.

   In the event that your Sketcher grid is not active, while in the sketcher, select the "Grid" icon ![Grid].

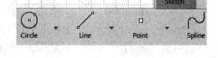

2- Select the "Circle" icon ![Circle] from the bottom row and draw a circle centered at the origin.

   Use the "Constraint" icon ![Constraint] from the bottom row to dimension it with a radius of R = 50 mm.

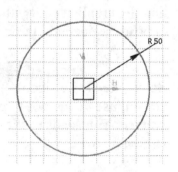

   Use the "Exit App" icon ![Exit App] to exit the sketcher and land in the 3D space.

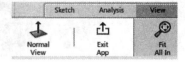

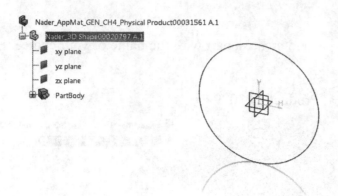

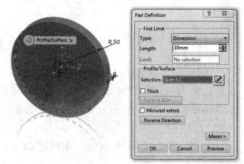

3- Select the "Pad" icon  from the bottom row to open the "Pad" dialogue box. For the "Selection," pick "Sketch.1" from the screen or from the tree. For "Length," input 10 mm.

The following disk is shown on your screen.

Note: At this point, you have two options. The first one is to create a "Pocket" on the front face, and then use the "Circular Pattern" to replicate it. The second option is to create a "Hole" on the front face and then replicate it by the "Circular Pattern." We choose the second option.

4- Select the "Hole" icon in the action bar. From the screen, use the cursor to pick the front face of the disk just created. This leads to the "Hole Definition" dialogue box shown below.

Select the "Positioned Sketch" icon from the dialogue box just opened. This will lead to the sketcher as shown on the right. An "x" is placed at the origin representing the default location of the center of the hole.

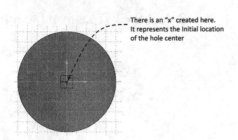

There is an "x" created here. It represents the Initial location of the hole center

Use the cursor to drag the "x" to a desired location and then create the appropriate dimension with the "Constraint" icon Constraint.

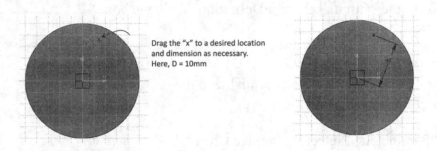

Drag the "x" to a desired location and dimension as necessary. Here, D = 10mm

Use the "Exit App" icon Exit App to exit the sketcher and land in the 3D space.

The screen will show the created hole of the correct size in a proper location.

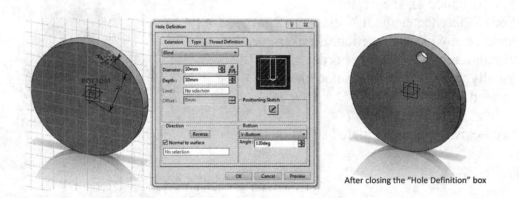

After closing the "Hole Definition" box

Note that there are many other options that could have been selected in order to fully customize the hole characteristics. In this problem, all default values

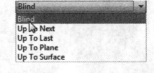

were accepted. The reader is advised to explore the other tabs "Type" and "Thread Definition."

5- Select the "Transform" tab from the group of icons in the bottom of the screen.

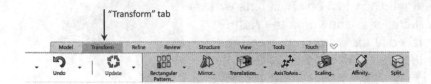

Choose the "Circular Pattern" 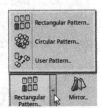 from the action bar.

This leads to the "Circular Pattern Definition" dialogue box shown below.

Note that there are many options available in the two tabs of the dialogue box.

For the "Parameters," select "Complete Crown."

For "Instance(s)," select 9.
For "Reference element," select the front face of the disk (or any circular section, for example, the circumferential bounding border of the disk).
Finally, for the "Object," select the Hole.1 just created.

See below for the completed selections.

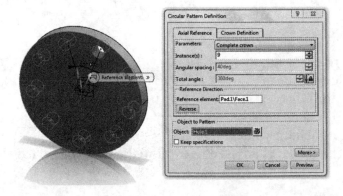

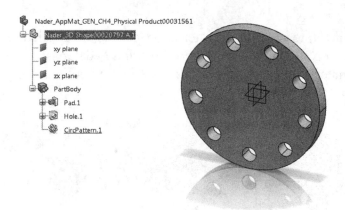

The task of creating the part is now complete. It should be noted that if in the above process, instead of the "Object" being "Hole.1," the default "Current Solid" was used, although the final part may look the same, the implications downstream may be severe, leading to erroneous results.

The effect of choosing different "Instance(s)" is shown below.

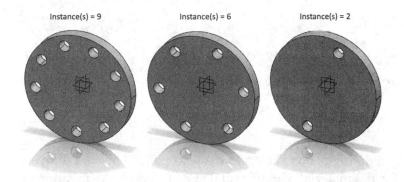

Down below, you see some other scenarios such as "Instances and Total Angle" instead of the "Complete crown."

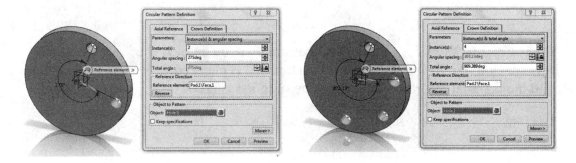

Applying Material Properties:

The main objective of this chapter was (is) to show how material properties are applied to a part. The assumption is that there are no suitable properties in the "cloud" database that can be used directly. Therefore, the material has to be created first and then applied.

The first task is to create a material property for this part. From the bottom row of icons (action bar), select the "Tools" tab.

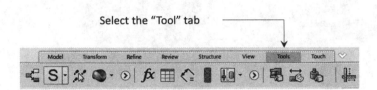

From the tool bar, choose the "Material Browser" icon . This opens up the section

menu as shown below. Follow the steps outlined to select "Create Material" .

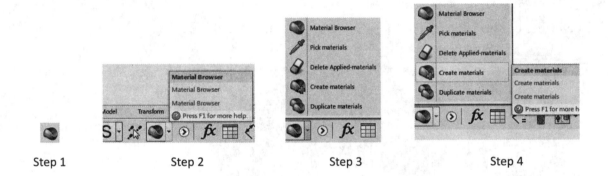

| Step 1 | Step 2 | Step 3 | Step 4 |

The selection of opens up a dialogue box shown in the next page. This box allows you to supply a proper name for the material, should you decide to do so. As mentioned earlier, our assumption is that you do not have a material of interest and would like to follow the steps to create it. It is a rather tedious process but needs to be clearly spelled out.

Select the "Create Material" icon. Make sure that you employ the "Add domain" pulldown menu to confirm that "Simulation Domain" is checked. Note that this creates a shell and the material information needs to be supplied later.

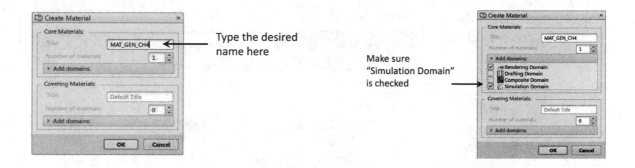

Once you close the dialogue box by clicking on "OK," you will find yourself in the material database and can identify the material that you just created, namely "MAT_GEN_CH4." The database screen is shown below.

Place the cursor on your created material in the database, right click and select "Apply." You still have to return to the screen where the geometry exists and continue. This necessitates the closure of the current screen (the database screen).

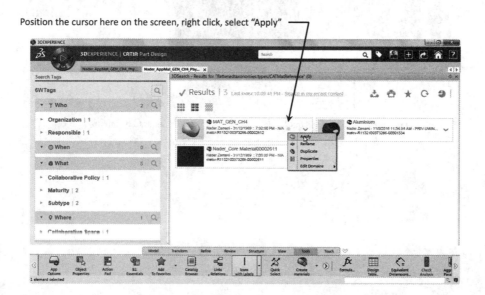

Click on the "X" on the top right margin of the database screen to close the window.

Close this window by clicking on "X."
Be careful not to close the App instead.

You will return to the geometry window; however, the shape of the cursor is modified as shown below.

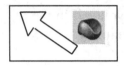

Place the cursor on the part, on the screen, or on the top branch of the tree and double click.

You will notice that the "Materials" branch is created at the very bottom of the tree as shown below. You can then use the cursor to pick the "Green" check mark to proceed.

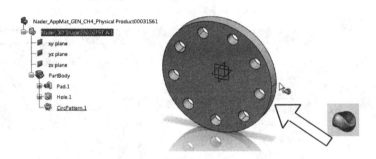

Select the "Green" check mark from this box.

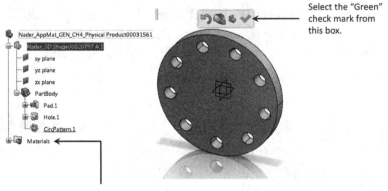

The created material has been assigned but this is just a shell, information needs to be inputted later.

Please note that the actual material properties are yet to be inputted. Expanding the "Materials" branch reveals two other branches. The location where the properties are inputted is the last branch "Nader_Material Simulation Domain00002980" as shown on the right.

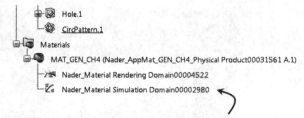

Input material properties by double clicking on this branch.

Double click on the last branch and follow the sequence of instructions below.

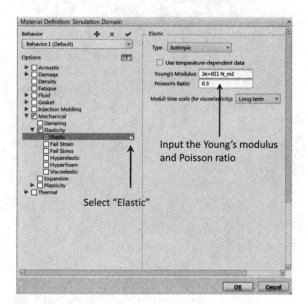

Step 1

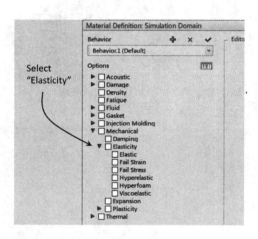

Select "Mechanical"

Step 2

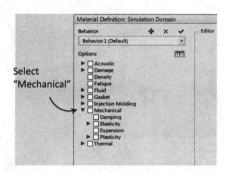

Select "Elasticity"

Step 3

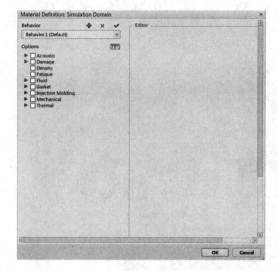

Input the Young's modulus and Poisson ratio

Select "Elastic"

Step 4

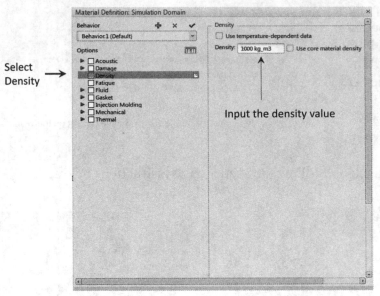

Select
Density

Input the density value

Step 5

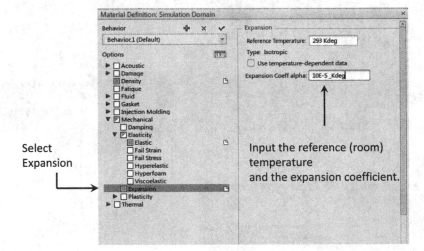

Select
Expansion

Input the reference (room)
temperature
and the expansion coefficient.

Step 6

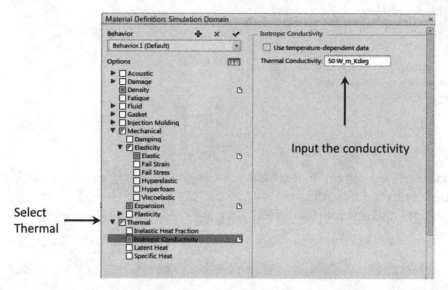

Step 7

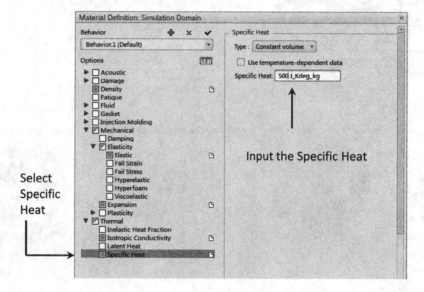

Step 8

Needless to say, rendering is an important aspect of a CAD software. In 3DEXPERIENCE this is achieved by the icons shown on the right. Use the "Shading with Materials" icon 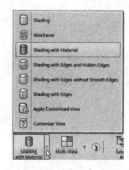 Shading with Material . This is shown on the next page.

Furthermore, to experiment with Rendering and lighting schemes, double click on the branch of the tree shown below.

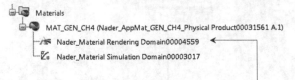

Double click for changing the rendering parameters

This leads to the dialogue box shown on the right. In order to experiment with lighting, drag the sliding bars shown below and observe the effect.

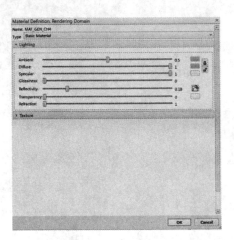

Drag these bars
to see the effect

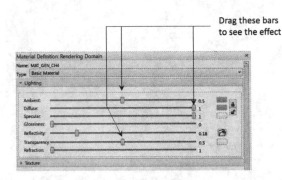

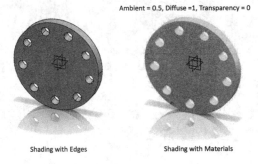

Ambient = 0.5, Diffuse =1, Transparency = 0   Ambient = 0, Diffuse = 1, Transparency = 0.5   Ambient = 0, Diffuse = 1, Transparency =0

Shading with Edges   Shading with Materials   Shading with Materials   Shading with Materials

A Closer Look at the Sketcher

Objective:

Now that you have successfully created some solid geometries, it is time to take a closer look at the Sketcher App and explore some of the functionalities not considered earlier.

Enter the Part Design App 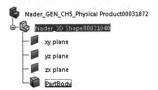 and create a part with the name of your choice. Here, the following name is used:

Nader_GEN_CH5_Physical Product00030794

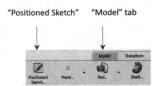

Some Comments about the "Positioned Sketch" Functionalities:

1- Select the "Positioned Sketch" icon 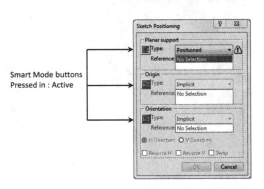 from the bottom row menu. Note that the "Positioned Sketch" is in the "Model" tab. This will open the dialogue box shown below.

In the left margin, there are three buttons that can be in a "pressed" or "un-pressed" state. These buttons are referred to as the "Smart Mode" selection. The best way to illustrate the role of "Smart Mode" is through an example.

"Positioned Sketch"   "Model" tab

Smart Mode buttons
Pressed in : Active

2- Ignoring dimensions, create a wedge whose base lies in the xy plane as shown.

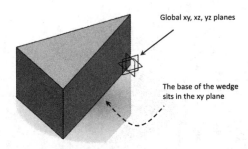

Global xy, xz, yz planes

The base of the wedge sits in the xy plane

3- Select the slanted face shown. Then select the "Positioned Sketch" icon 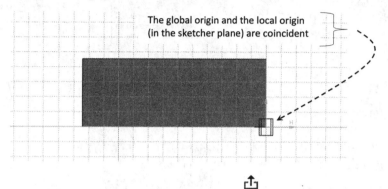 from the action bar (*in the order just mentioned, i.e., first the face and then the icon*). This will land you in the sketcher but the origin of the sketcher plane is coincident with the global origin as shown below.

The global origin and the local origin (in the sketcher plane) are coincident

Without doing any work exit the sketcher ⬆ Exit App .

4- Now select the "Positioned Sketch" icon *first* (without any further selection). Make sure that the "Smart Mode" button *is not* in the "pressed" state.

The "Smart Mode" button **not** in the "pressed" state.

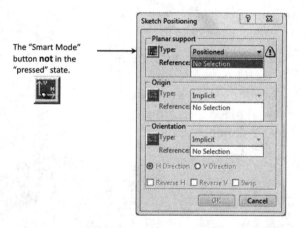

5- With the "Smart Mode" button **not** in the "pressed" state, select the slanted Face.

With the "Smart Mode" button **not** in the "pressed" state, select the slanted face

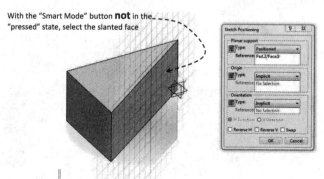

6- Note that regardless of whether the other two "Smart Mode" buttons (the ones in the "Origin" and the "Orientation" sections) were pressed or not, once the previous step is completed, they go into the "un-pressed" mode.

After completing step 5, these two buttons go into the "un pressed" state.

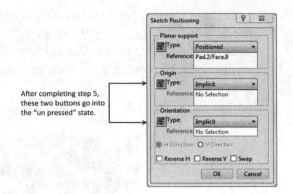

Use the pulldown menu and select the "Projection point."

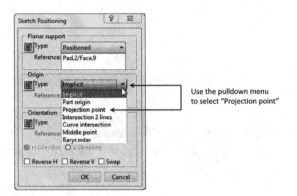

Use the pulldown menu to select "Projection point"

For the "Projection point" select the vertex of the wedge as shown. This will place the origin of the sketcher plane at the vertex picked.

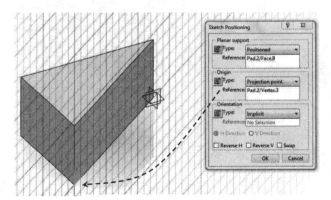

For the "Projection point," select this vertex of the wedge

Use the pulldown menu and select the "Through point."

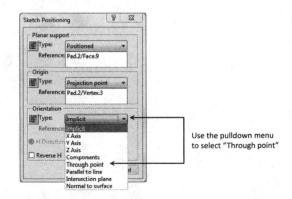

Use the pulldown menu to select "Through point"

For the "Through point," select the vertex of the wedge as shown. This will rotate the sketcher coordinate system to make the horizontal axis pass through the selected vertex.

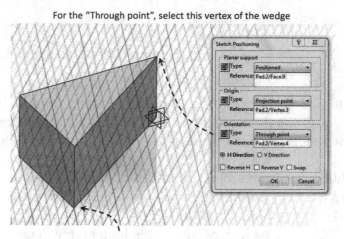

For the "Through point", select this vertex of the wedge

Note that the sketcher coordinate system has been rotated

Once you click on "OK," you land in the sketcher with the selected orientation with respect to the wedge.

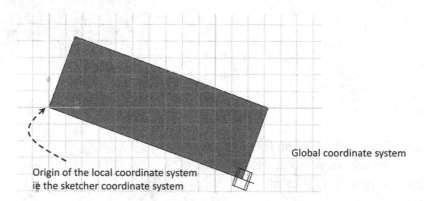

Global coordinate system

Origin of the local coordinate system
is the sketcher coordinate system

To see the implication of these steps, draw a rectangle in the sketcher and exit to see how it looks on the face of the wedge. The outcome is shown below.

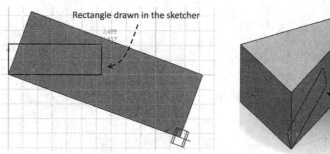

Rectangle drawn in the sketcher

Rectangle's orientation on the face of the wedge

Delete the created wedge to start with a clean slate.

The Concept of Construction Elements:

On a plane of your choice, enter the sketcher, draw a line and a spline as shown.

For the spline, use the icon 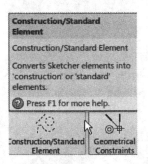 **Spline** . The actual dimensions are not important. The intention is to find the mirror of the spline with respect to the drawn line. The sole purpose of the line is to use it for reflection and does not have any direct purpose in the 3D model generation. Such entities are called "Construction" elements.

Although it is possible to do the mirroring with respect to the line as it is, we choose to turn it into a "Construction" element. Select the "Construction Standard Element" icon

Construction/Standard Element . This icon resides in the bottom row in the sketcher.

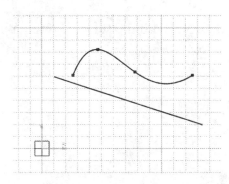

Construction/Standard Element
Construction/Standard Element
Converts Sketcher elements into 'construction' or 'standard' elements.
ⓘ Press F1 for more help.
Construction/Standard Element   Geometrical Constraints

After the icon is selected, pick the line on the screen which will immediately turn into a dashed line. Dashed lines/curves mean that they are construction elements.

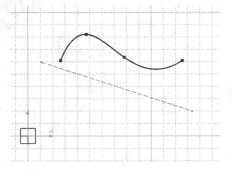

Select the "Mirror" icon **Mirror** from the bottom row. You are prompted to select the spline (the object to be mirrored) followed by the mirroring element (in this case the line). The result is shown on the right.

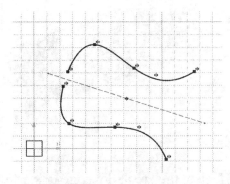

Exit the sketcher 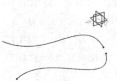 .

Select the sketch just created followed by the "Pad" icon 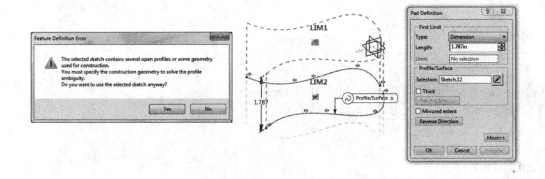 . You are faced with the following problematic message.

The issue seems to be the presence of open curves in the created sketch. This needs to be resolved in the sketcher.

Pad/Pocketing of Open Curves:

On a plane of your choice, enter the sketcher, draw an <u>open profile</u> such as the one shown on the right. The dimensions are not relevant.

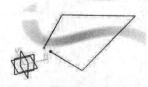

Exit the sketcher 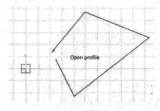 and try to "Pad" it.

You are faced with the "Feature Definition Error" dialogue box. This stems from the fact that in principle, an open profile cannot be padded or pocketed. One has to return to the sketcher and close the gap.

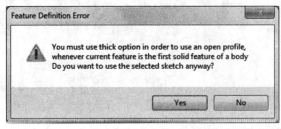

Select "NO" and cancel the "Pad" dialogue box.

Return to the sketch just created. This can be done by double clicking on the actual sketch which resides in space, or double clicking on the branch of the tree containing the sketch.

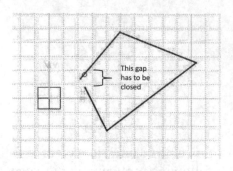

In the present problem, the gap is big enough that it can be identified and closed manually. One way to achieve this is first to select the two end points (Ctrl key down while doing multiple selection).

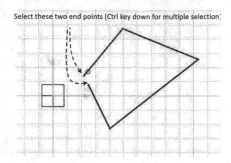

Use the "Constraint…" icon ![icon] from the expanded menu and check the "Coincidence" box.

This will close the gap but if it is too small to detect with the naked eye, it is difficult to implement. Cancel the dialogue box so that the second method can be explained for the same profile.

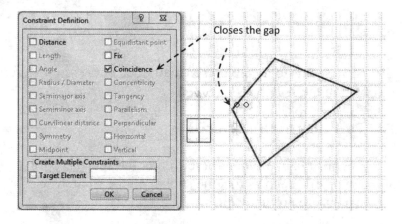

Select the "Analysis" tab from the bottom row of icons.

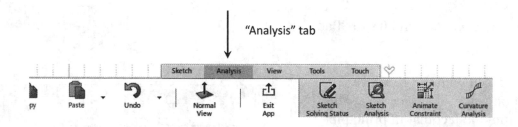

Select the "Sketch Analysis" icon ![Sketch Analysis] from the bottom row. This leads to the dialogue box displayed in the next page.

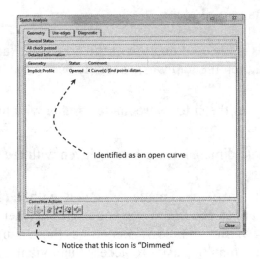

Identified as an open curve

Notice that this icon is "Dimmed"

Within the "Sketch Analysis" dialogue box, select the entry in the Geometry column labeled "Implicit Profile."

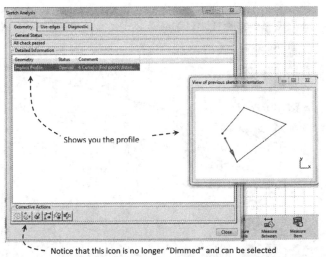

Shows you the profile

Notice that this icon is no longer "Dimmed" and can be selected

Select the "Close Opened Profile" icon from the list of "Corrective Actions" in the bottom left margin

. This closes the open profile.

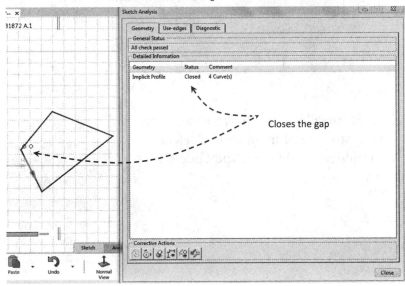

Closes the gap

Constraints in a Sketch:

This is the continuation of the previous example where an open profile was created and then the gap was closed by one of the two proposed methods. After closing the gap, two of the sides were made parallel with the icon ; two length dimensions and one angle dimension were introduced with the icon . Finally, the bottom left vertex of the profile was made coincident with the horizontal axis with . All these constraints are stored in the tree under the sketcher branch and they are accounted for in the drawing as shown below. Sometimes these constraints may have to be edited or deleted and it may be easier to access them via the tree.

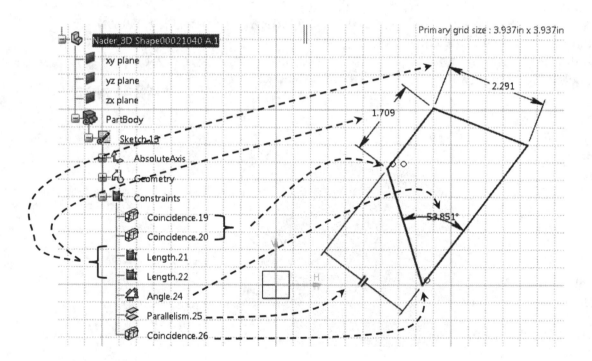

To clean off the clutter of the constraints on the screen, any one of them can be selected and then hidden. Right click and Hide/Show as shown.

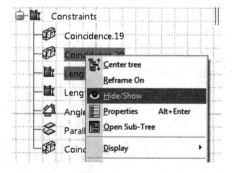

Over Constraining in a Sketch:

On a plane of your choice, enter the sketcher, draw a rectangle and dimension as shown. Try drawing the rectangle roughly as it is shown, i.e., the sides not being on the local axis.

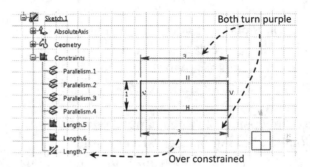

Now impose another dimension on the horizontal edge as indicated. You will see that both horizontal dimensions turn purple. This is an indication that the sketch becomes over-constrained. In fact, the tree shows that this last dimension is crossed out.

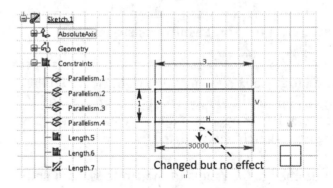

Even if you try to change the second dimension on the screen from 3 units to 30000 units, although the number changes, the length of the rectangle remains the same.
Next, delete the last dimension which caused the sketch to become over-constrained.

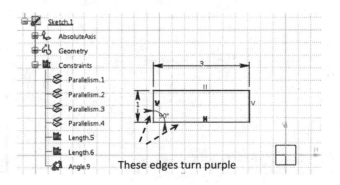

Try creating an angle dimension between the left vertical and the bottom horizontal edges. You will see that once again, the sketch becomes over-constrained and will turn purple. The reason being that the rectangle drawn already imposes that condition. Delete the angle dimension to proceed.

Finally, create the two dimensions
between the edges of the rectangle and
the horizontal and vertical axis of the
sketcher as shown. You will notice that
the entire rectangle turns "**Green**." This
is an indication the sketch is fully
constrained.

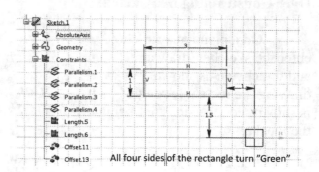

All four sides of the rectangle turn "Green"

Editing Many Constraints Simultaneously in a Sketch:

On a plane of your choice, enter the
sketcher, draw a rectangle and circle and
dimension them as shown. Use units of your
choice.

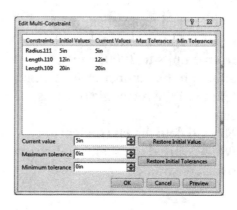

These dimensions can be changed one at a time
by double clicking on them. Every time you
change one of these dimensions, the entire sketch gets updated.

The alternative is to change them all at the same
time. Select the "Edit Multi-Constraint" icon

![Edit Multi-Constraint] from the bottom row. This opens
the dialogue box shown on the right where all the
dimensions in the sketch are listed. Any one of
them can be changed and upon closing the window,
the entire sketch gets updated.

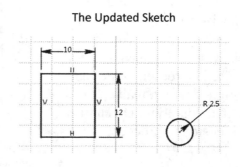

Let us change the radius of the circle to 2.5in and
the vertical edge of the rectangle to 10in. Upon
closing the window, the updated sketch appears.

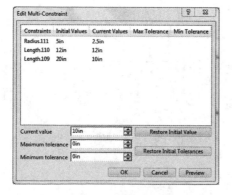

The Updated Sketch

Projecting onto a Sketching Plane:

Consider the situation shown on the right. The intention is to project the circle describing the bottom of the cylinder onto the top face of the block, change the radius of the projected circle, and use it to make a pocket in the block.

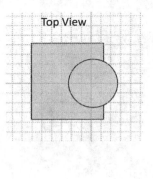
Perspective View

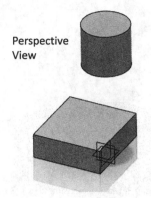
Top View

Select the top face of the block and enter the sketcher .

Rotate the sketch plane to have a better idea of what transpires in the next several steps.

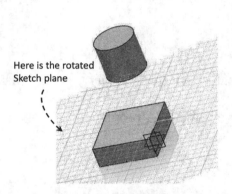
Here is the rotated Sketch plane

Select the "Project 3D Elements" from the bottom row of icons and then the circle at the bottom of the cylinder.

The result is the dialogue box shown on the right. Close it by clicking "OK."

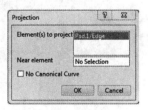

This will project the circle onto the face of the block as shown. Because this is a projection, the size of the circle cannot be changed. The solution is to "Isolate" this circle, and then try to change it.

Select the "Isolate" icon and pick the projected circle.

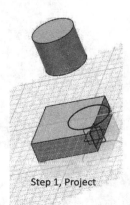
Step 1, Project

Dimension the circle, and then you are allowed to change the dimension. This could not have been done without the "Isolation" step.

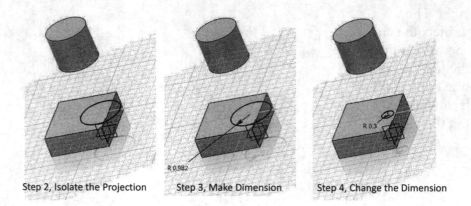

Step 2, Isolate the Projection   Step 3, Make Dimension   Step 4, Change the Dimension

Finally, exit the sketcher ⬆ Exit App and make a pocket with Pocket....

Here is the final product.

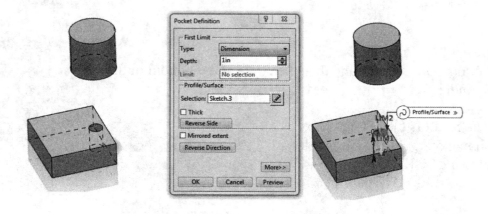

Exercise 1

In this exercise you will be exploring the "Animate Constraint" icon 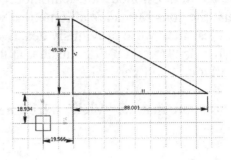. Enter the sketcher and create a right triangle as shown below. Dimension the sides of the triangle along with the location of the specific vertex shown.

While in the sketcher, make sure that the "Analysis" tab is active.

Analysis
tab

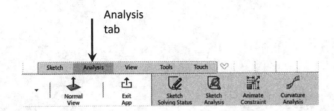

Next, select the bottom horizontal dimension followed by the "Animate Constraint" icon

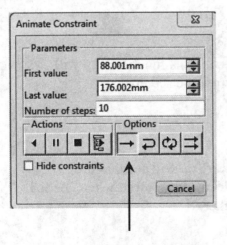. This immediately leads you to the "Animate Constraint" dialogue box shown below.

Select dimension from
screen followed by the icon

Animate Constraint

Parameters

First value: 88.001mm

Last value: 176.002mm

Number of steps: 10

Actions **Options**

◄ ‖ ■ | → ⇄ ⇌ ⇥

☐ Hide constraints

Cancel

Forward Animation

Select the "Play" button and observe the animation.

Exercise 2

In this exercise you will be exploring some icons in the "View" tab of the sketcher. Enter the sketcher and create a rectangle as shown below with the sides dimensioned. The actual dimensioned values are not relevant. Note that the constraints are automatically being tracked (unless they were previously deactivated). The symbols "H" and "V" indicate that these sides are horizontal and vertical.

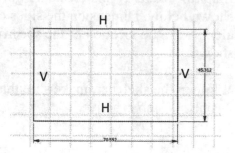

Make sure that the "View" tab of the action bar is active.

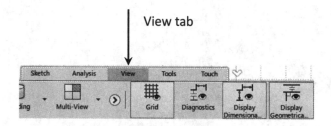

Select the "Grid" icon [ ]; you will see that this will hide and restore the background grid.

Next select the "Display Dimensiona…" icon [ ]. This functionality will conveniently hide/restore the dimensions collectively from the screen.

Finally, select "Display Geometrical…" icon [ ]. You will see that the "geometrical Constraints" such as "H" and "V" are hidden and restored when needed. These icons can be very helpful when working in sketcher.

Making a Piston

Objective:

In this chapter, you will construct a simple model of a piston. The dimensions of the part are shown below and they are in inches.

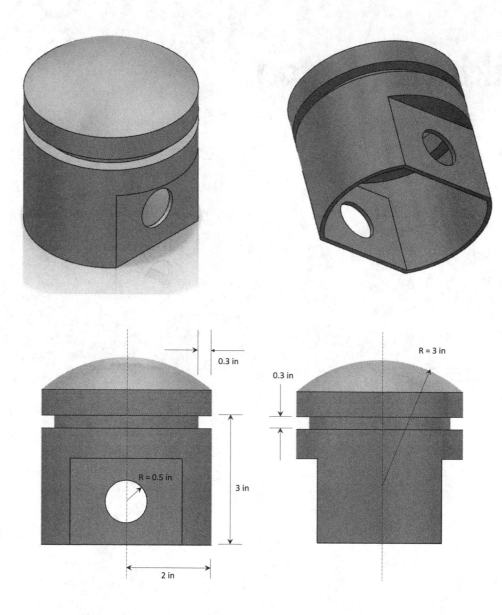

Creating the Piston:

Before you start the work, change the units of length to inches. The procedure was explained in Chapter 1.

Enter the Part Design App  and create a part with the name of your choice. Here, the following name was used:

Nader_Piston_CH6_Physical Product00031930

Select the yz plane and enter the sketcher.

Use the "Profile" icon to create the sketch shown with the appropriate dimensions.

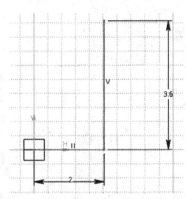

Use the "Arc" icon to draw the arc shown whose center is on the vertical coordinate system with a radius of 3 in.

Exit the sketcher.

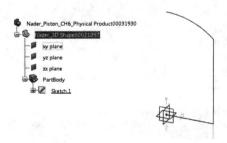

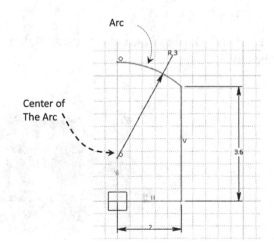

Select the "Shaft" icon 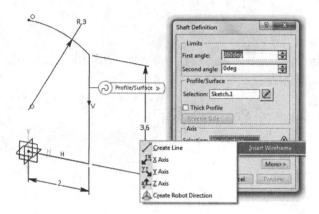 and pick Sketch.1 for the support. For the "Axis," place the cursor in that box, right click, and select the Z axis.

Upon closing the dialogue box, the shafted piston appears on the screen.

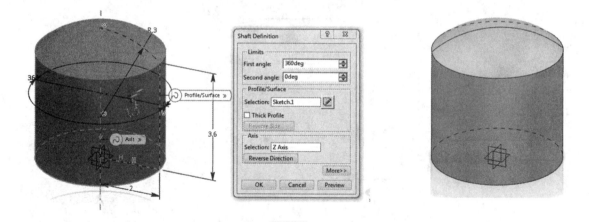

Select the yz plane and enter the sketcher 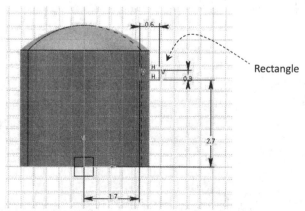. Draw the rectangle and dimension it as shown.

Exit the sketcher 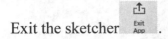 .

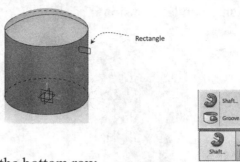

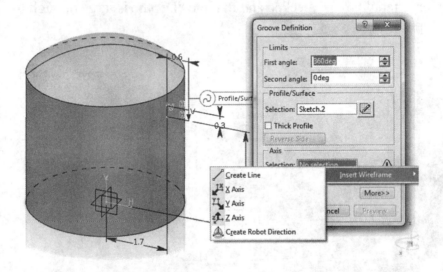

Pick the "Groove" icon from the bottom row.

For the "Profile" choose "Sketch.2"; for the Axis, place the cursor in that location, right click, and select "Z Axis."

The resulting groove is shown below.

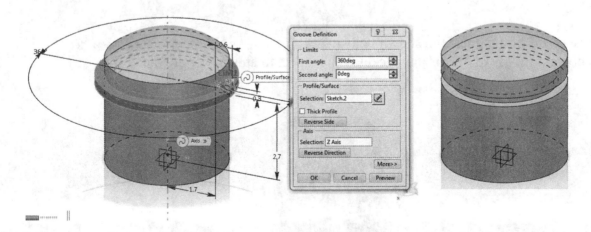

Select the yz plane and enter the sketcher 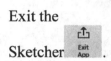.
Draw the rectangle and dimension it as shown.

Exit the

Sketcher .

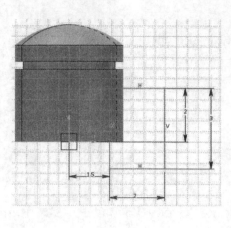

Pick the rectangle just drawn, and use the "Pocket" icon 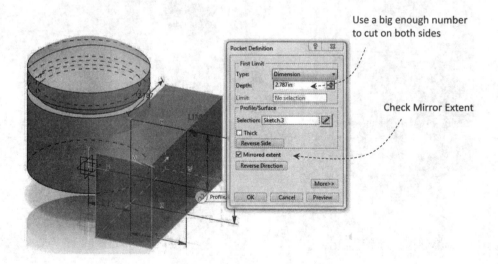 to make a pocket. Make sure the "Mirror extent" box is checked and that the "Depth" is large enough to completely cut the piston.

The result of the pocket is shown below.
The next task is to mirror the pocket with respect to an appropriate plane (i.e., xz).

The "Mirror" icon 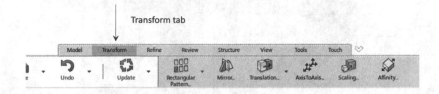 is in the Transform tab of the bottom row.

For the "Mirroring element," select the zx plane and for the "Object to mirror" select "Pocket.1" from the screen or the tree.

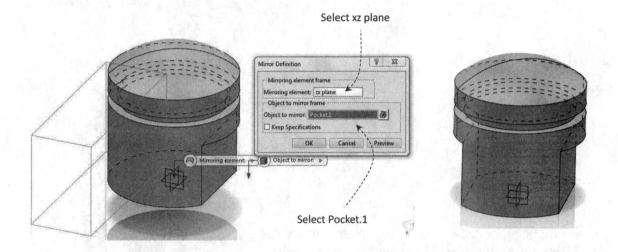

Select the flat rectangular face on the piston and enter the sketcher.

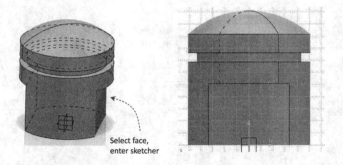

On this sketch plane, draw a circle Circle of radius R = 1in and make it centered. If the center of the circle is on the vertical axis, it becomes automatically centered horizontally. To center it vertically, make the selections shown below, in the order shown. Keep in mind that multiple selection requires the Ctrl key being down during selection.

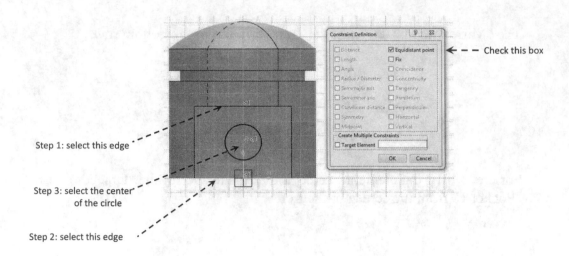

Step 1: select this edge

Step 3: select the center
of the circle

Step 2: select this edge

Check this box

Exit the Sketcher 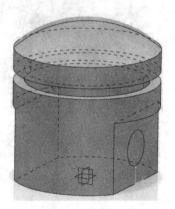 .

Select the circle just drawn, and use the "Pocket" icon
to make a pocket. One way to ensure that it cuts
completely through the part is to use a large enough
"Depth," or for "Type" use "Up to Last."

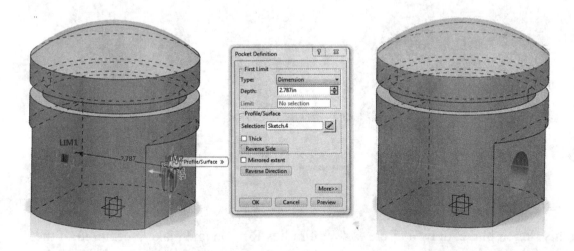

The next step is to hollow out the piston. This is done by using the "Shell" icon .

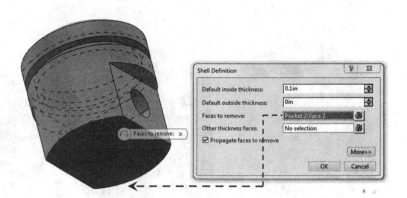

For the "Face to remove" select the bottom of the piston and change the default inside thickness to 0.1 in.

The result of shelling is shown on the right. As you can see, the piston has been hollowed out but there is an extra surface that should have been removed.

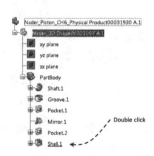

This face should have Been removed too.

Double click on the "Shell" branch in the tree to open the dialogue box.

Already the bottom of the cylinder was selected, now you have to select the curved inside surface of the pocket (hole).

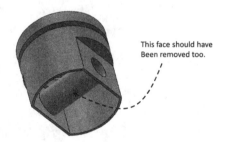

Double click

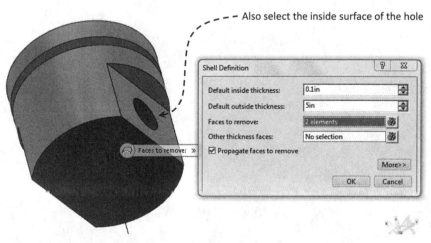

Also select the inside surface of the hole

Several different views of the piston are shown below.

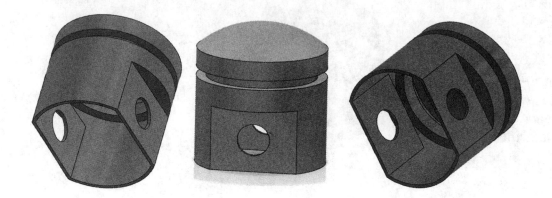

The final tree is also provided below.

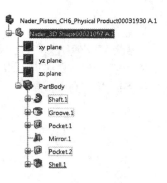

Chapter 7

Rib & Slot
vs Pad & Pocket

Objective:

In view of the fact the "Pad" and "Pocket" operations are widely used in CAD modeling, the objective of this chapter is to have a closer look at these two operations and observe some of their limitations. These limitations can be overcome by using the "Rib" and "Slot" operations to some extent. Although units and dimensions are specified in the chapter development, these are not critical and the reader can proceed as desired. The concept of "Geometrical Sets" is also introduced along the way.

Geometrical Sets:

First use the procedure outlined in chapter 1 to change your length units to mm.

Enter the Part Design App 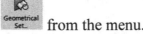 and create a part with the name of your choice. Here, the following name is used:

Nader_GEN_CH7_Physical Product00031990

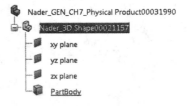

Select the "Structure" tab from the bottom menu.

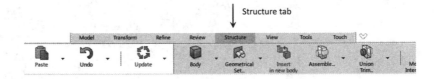

Click on the "Geometrical Set" icon 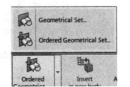 from the menu.

This leads to the dialogue box shown.

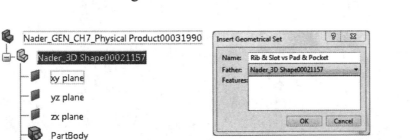

Specify the name "Rib & Slot vs Pad & Pocket" for this geometrical set. You will create several entities and they will be stored in this set. This is a good way to organize your work.

Select the yz plane and enter the sketcher 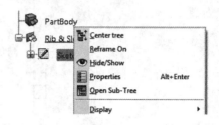.
In the sketcher, draw a rectangle as shown with
the indicated dimensions 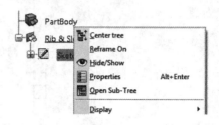. Remember the
unit is mm.

Exit the sketcher 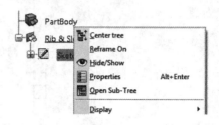. The default name
"Sketch.1" has been assigned to this drawing.
Since there will be other sketches in this
geometrical set, it is better to give each a
unique name. Position the cursor on "Sketch.1"
in the tree, right click and select "Properties."

The "Properties" dialogue box opens which
has four tabs. Select the "Feature Properties"
tab where you can input a name of your
choice. For the "Feature Name," type
"Rectangle of the Base." Click on "OK" and
you will see the new name appearing in the
tree.

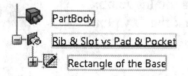

The plan is to create another sketch on the yz plane. Select the yz
plane once again and enter the sketcher 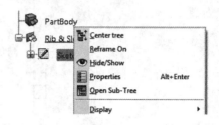. Use the "Polygon"
icon  to draw a polygon as shown.

Use the dimensions shown and make sure that the center of polygon lies on the top edge
of the rectangle of the earlier sketch and centered horizontally on the edge. Note that
although the rectangle from the first sketch is also visible here, it does not belong to the
sketch you are currently working with. You will soon see that there is a need to return to
this sketch and change the size of the polygon.

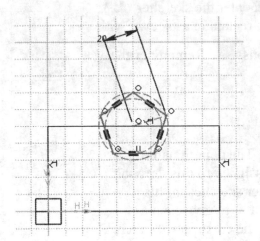

Using the procedure described in the previous page, change the name of this sketch from "Sketch.2" to "Pentagon."

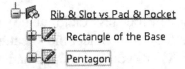

The next task is to create a plane parallel to the xy plane with an offset of 150 mm above it.

Pick the "Plane" icon  from the menu. There are many different ways to create a plane. Using the pulldown menu in the dialogue box, you can explore these choices. For the "Reference" pick the "xy plane" from the screen or the tree. For "Plane type" use "Offset from plane." For the "Offset" type 150 mm.

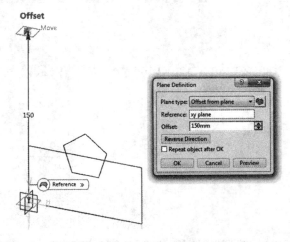

Upon pressing "OK" the plane is shown on the screen and the tree.

The plane just constructed 150mm above the xy plane

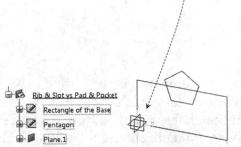

You will be creating two new sketches on this plane. They will be a line with a given orientation, and a spline.

First let us create the line.

Select the "Plane.1" just created

and enter the sketcher 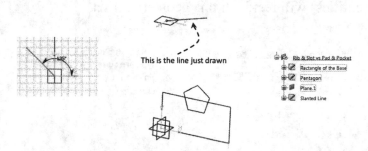. In this sketch, draw a line at 135 degrees with the horizontal axis. There is no specific significance to 135 degrees; it was selected arbitrarily. After completing the task, exit the sketcher and rename it to be "Slanted Line."

Next, the spline sketch will be created.

Select the "Plane.1" created earlier and enter the sketcher 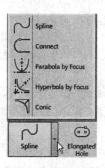. In the

sketch use the "Spline" icon ⟳ Spline to draw a spline roughly as what is shown below. There is nothing special about drawing a spline; you can draw another curve if you wish to do so.

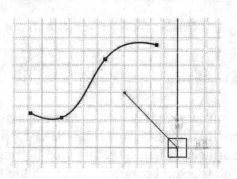

Exit the sketcher and rename the sketch just
drawn to "Spline."

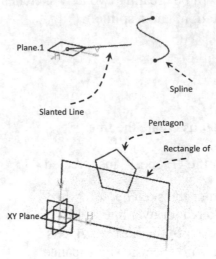

A quick glance of the tree shows that all the
entities constructed reside within the
geometrical set named "Rib & Slot vs Pad &
Pocket." Furthermore, this geometrical set is
underlined. The underlining implies that
whatever is being done (including creating
entities) will reside in this geometrical set.

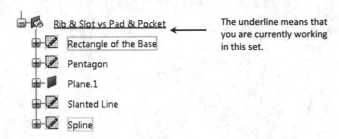

The value of a geometrical set is that the entities within it can be used by other operations
such as Pad, Pocket, Rib, Shaft, etc., repeatedly. It also displays all the entities quickly
and as a group. In the next few pages, you will be experimenting with these sketches to
perform certain operations.

Use Pad to Create the Base:

From the tree, select the sketch named
"Rectangle of the Base" followed by

the "Pad" icon . You are
immediately faced with a "Warning"
message.

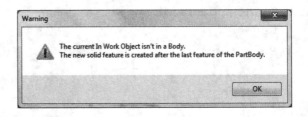

This warning message does not prevent you from proceeding with the Pad operation;
however, it may be a good idea to know where it is coming from. In 3DEXPERIENCE,
geometrical sets are made of wirframes and surfaces. The fact that the geometrical set
was underlined implies the "Pad" object, which is a solid part, is to reside in the set.
However, geometrical sets ordinarily do not hold solid geometries.

One way to have avoided this warning was to
return to the "PartBody" by leaving the
geometrical set and then perform the "Pad"
operation.

Put the cursor on the branch of the tree labeled
"PartBody," right click and select "Define In
Work Object."

By doing so, the "PartBody" branch is
underlined and you can carry out the "Pad"
operation without any warning messages.

As mentioned earlier, you could have ignored
the warning and proceeded.

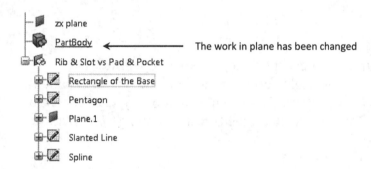

From the tree, select the sketch named "Rectangle of the Base" followed by the "Pad"
icon 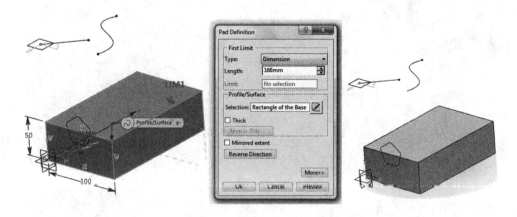.

For the "Profile," select "Rectangle of the Base" and for the "Length" input 166 mm.

Default Padding of the Pentagon:

From the tree select the sketch named "Pentagon" followed by the "Pad" icon 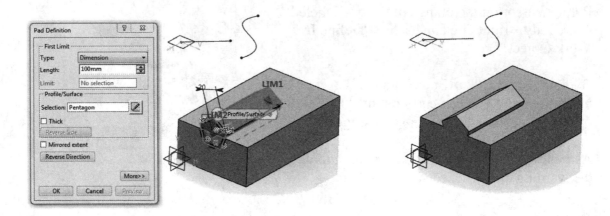 .
For the "Length" input 100 mm. This is not surprising as you have used it many times.

Double click the "Pad" from the tree for the same dialogue box to open.
Click on the "More" button at the bottom right corner of the dialogue box to expand it.
On the right side, uncheck box "Normal to profile" which then allows you to choose a
straight line. For this "Reference," select "Slanted Line" created in the geometrical set.

For "Reference" select the "Slanted Line"

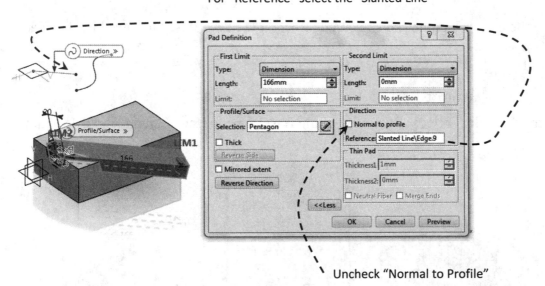

Uncheck "Normal to Profile"

Therefore, the direction of the "Pad" does not have to be perpendicular to the profile.

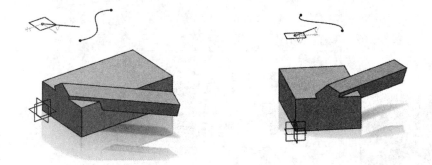

Default Pocketing of the Pentagon:

From the tree select the sketch named "Pentagon" followed by the "Pocket" icon Pocket.
For the "Length" input 100 mm. This is not surprising as have used pocket many times.

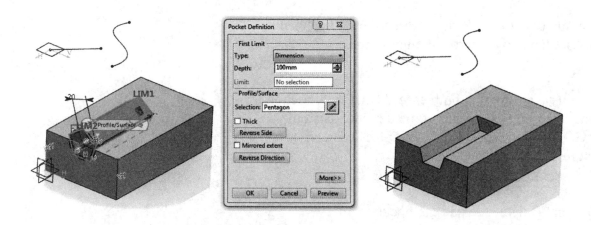

Double click on the "Pocket" from the tree for the same dialogue box to open.
Click on the "More" button at the bottom right corner of the dialogue box to expand it.
On the right side, uncheck box "Normal to profile" which then allows you to choose a straight line. For this "Reference," select "Slanted Line" created in the geometrical set.

For "Reference" select the "Slanted Line"

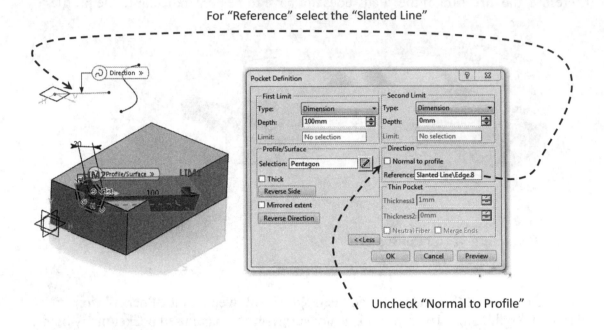

Uncheck "Normal to Profile"

As in the case of the Pad, the direction of the "Pocket" does not have to be perpendicular to the profile.

The only restriction in both cases is that the direction is along a straight line. What if the direction is along a curve? This is where "Rib" and "Slot" come in the picture.

You can "Delete" the pad the pocket generated without effecting the corresponding sketches.
All that needs to be done is selecting the entity from the tree. Right click, and select "Delete."

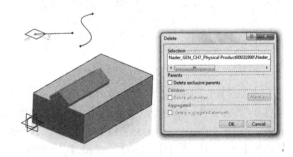

Ribbing/Slotting of the Pentagon along the Spline:

From the tree select the sketch named "Pentagon" followed by the

"Rib" icon .

The "Rib" dialogue box opens. For the "Profile" select "Pentagon" from the tree. For the "Center curve" select the "Spline." The size of the Pentagon and the curvature of the spline are such that the ribbing operation fails as shown in the "Feature Definition Error" window below.

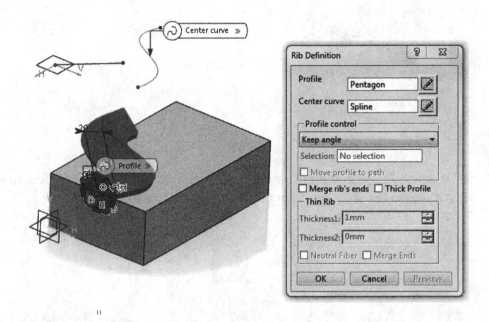

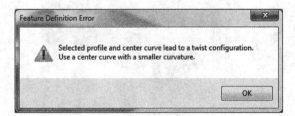

This issue was mentioned earlier. The solution is
either to resize the Pentagon or the Spline. We
choose to do the former. Close the "Rib"
dialogue box.
Double click on the Pentagon sketch in the
geometrical set to land in the sketcher. Change
the dimension of the Pentagon from 20 mm to 10
mm as shown. Exit the sketcher.

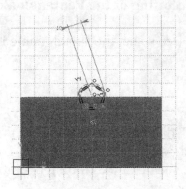

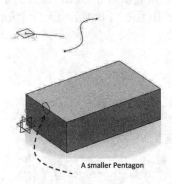

A smaller Pentagon

 Try the "Rib" icon 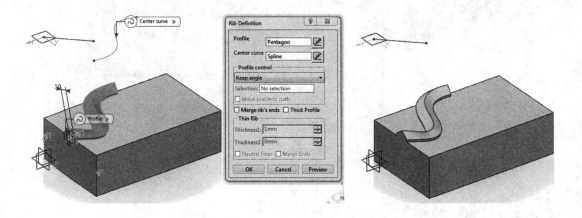 again with the same picks as in the previous page. This time
there are no error messages and the ribbing operation is successful.

Also try the "Slot" icon ![Slot] which leads to the configuration below.

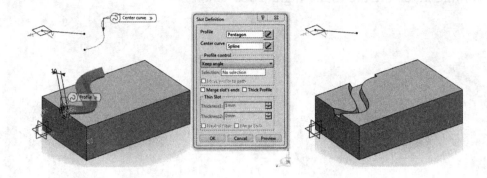

Exercise 1:

Using the "Rib" command, create the following drawer handle.

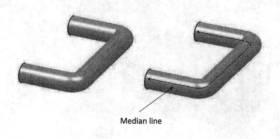

Median line

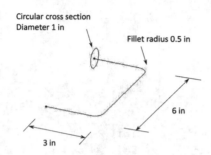

Circular cross section
Diameter 1 in

Fillet radius 0.5 in

6 in

3 in

Exercise 2:

Using the "Rib" command along with "Circular Pattern," create the solid object. Choose
your own dimensions.

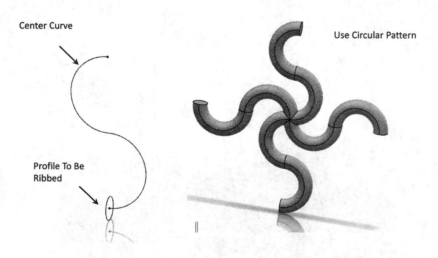

Center Curve

Use Circular Pattern

Profile To Be
Ribbed

Multi Pad and Multi Pocket

Objective:

The purpose of this chapter is to introduce two very important tools known as the Multi Pad and the Multi Pocket features in 3DEXPERIENCE. These are the close counterparts of Pad and Pocket already visited. The "Multi" operations are very efficient and effective approaches to model creation. The dimensions are irrelevant in the present chapter and therefore left to the reader. The two models that will be created are displayed below.

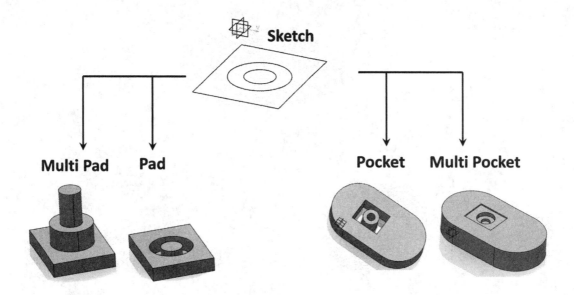

Creating the Geometrical Set and the Sketch:

First use the procedure outlined in chapter 1 to change your length units to mm.

Enter the Part Design App 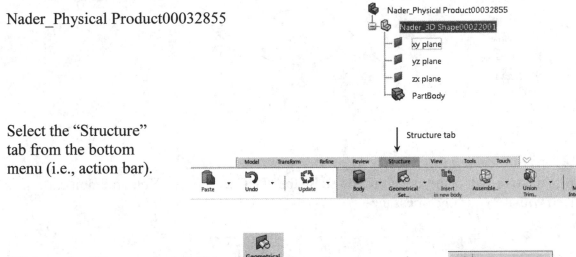 and create a part with the name of your choice. Here, the following name is used:

Nader_Physical Product00032855

Select the "Structure" tab from the bottom menu (i.e., action bar).

Structure tab

Click on the "Geometrical Set" icon 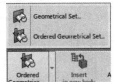 from the menu and give it the name "Three curves."

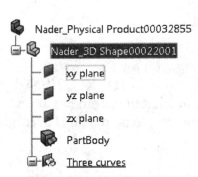

Notice that the geometrical set "Three curves" just created is underlined. This means that any wireframe or surfaces that are created at this point will end up in this set.

Select the xy plane and enter the sketcher . In the sketcher, draw two concentric circles enclosed within a rectangle as shown. The dimensions are not important.

Exit the sketcher 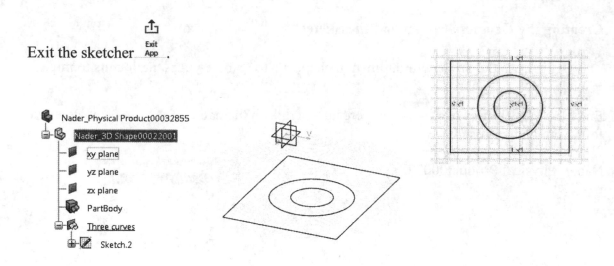.

From the tree, select the sketch followed by the "Pad" icon 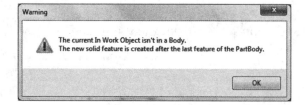. You are immediately faced with a "Warning" message.

This warning message does not prevent you from proceeding with the Pad operation; however, it may be a good idea to know where it is coming from. In 3DEXPERIENCE, geometrical sets are made of wirframes and surfaces. The fact that the geometrical set was underlined implies the the "Pad" object, which is a solid part to be made, is to reside in the set.

One way to have avoided this warning was to return to the "PartBody" by leaving the geometrical set and then perform the "Pad" operation.

Put the cursor on the branch of the tree labeled "PartBody," right click and select "Define In Work Object."

By doing so, the "PartBody" branch is underlined and you can carry out the "Pad" operation without any warning messages.

We choose to ignore the "Warning" message and proceed with the padding operation. The pad operation results in the geometry shown on the next page which may not be what was intended.

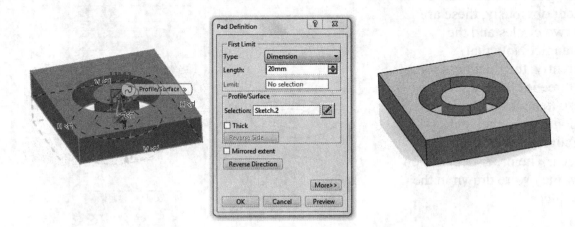

Now, suppose that you do not want to delete this pad. You can "Deactivate" it from the model. Select Pad.1 from the tree, and right click "Deactivate."

One should keep in mind that there is a significant difference between "Hide," "Delete" and "Deactivate."

After deactivating Pad.1, it no longer appears on the screen.

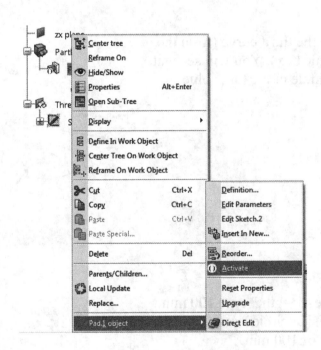

Creating the Multi Pad:

Select the "Multi Pad" icon  from the menu which leads to the dialogue box shown on the next page.

Here, you see three curves
listed; obviously, these are
the two circles and the
rectangle. Note that
currently, the thickness for
all three is "0." By selecting
these items from the
dialogue box, they get
highlighted in blue on the
screen. The order depends on
how they were drawn in the
first place.

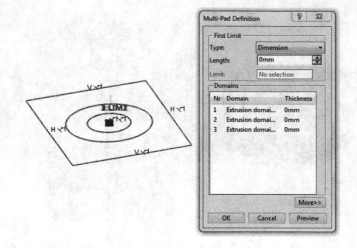

Select the third curve (from the
dialogue box). You will see that
the middle circle turns blue.

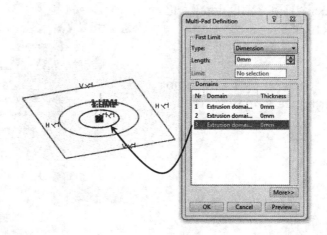

For the "length," type 100 mm.
The inside circle rises to have a
height of 100 mm.

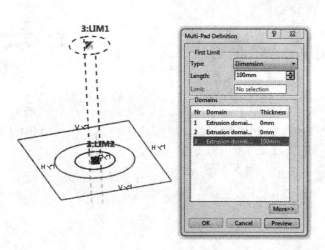

Next select the second curve (from the dialogue box); you will see that the outer circle turns blue.

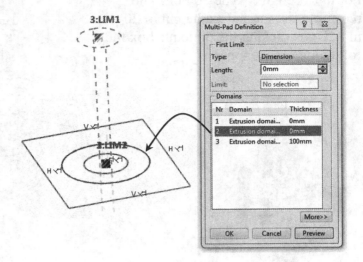

For the "length," type 50 mm. The outer circle rises to have a height of 50 mm.

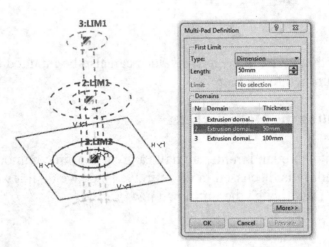

Finally select the first curve (from the dialogue box); you will see that the rectangle turns blue.

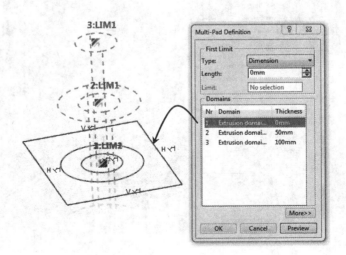

For the "Length," type 20 mm. The rectangle rises to have a height of 20 mm. Upon closing the dialogue box the following object appears.

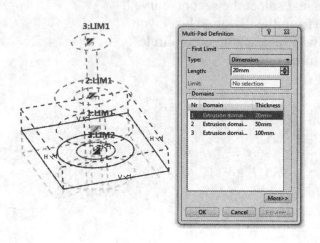

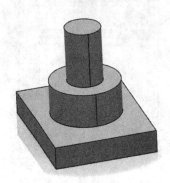

Note that zero and negative values can also be inputted for the height and the reader is encouraged to try them.

Creating the Multi Pocket:

Multi pocket and multi pad have a great deal in common but due to their importance the procedure is discussed in its entirety. Since we do not want to delete the multi pad, we will "Deactivate" the multi pad just created.

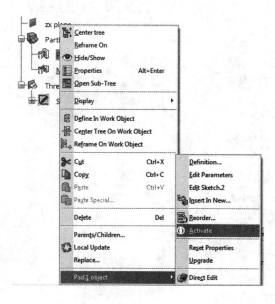

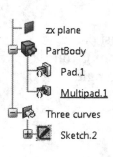

To make the visualization of the process easier, we will describe both pocket and multi pocket by performing them on a base. Let us switch to the geometrical set. Select the set "Three curves," right click and pick "Define In Work Object."

Note that the branch "Three curves" becomes underlined. So any wireframe and surface that is created will reside in the above geometrical set.

Select the xy plane and enter the sketcher Positioned Sketch . In the sketcher use the "Elongated Hole" icon Elongated Hole to draw the following sketch. This will be Sketch.3 in our tree. The dimensions are not important.

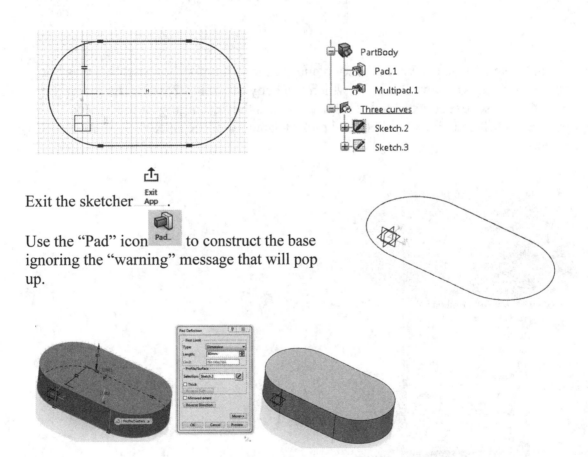

Exit the sketcher Exit App .

Use the "Pad" icon Pad to construct the base ignoring the "warning" message that will pop up.

The next step is to copy Sketch.2 and paste it in the geometrical set. This will create a copy of the original sketch which can be used in future.

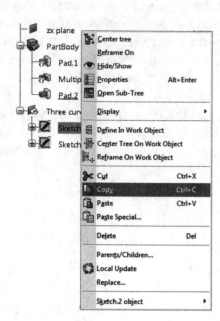

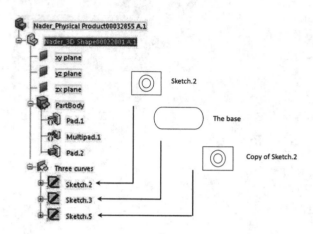

Recall that Sketch.2 was drawn on the xy plane; i.e., the "Support" of Sketch.2 was the xy plane. However, we want Sketch.5 (which is a copy of Sketch.2) to be drawn on the top face of the base just constructed. This necessitates the "Changing of the Sketch Support." Select Sketch.5, right click, and pick "Changing of the Sketch Support" as shown below.

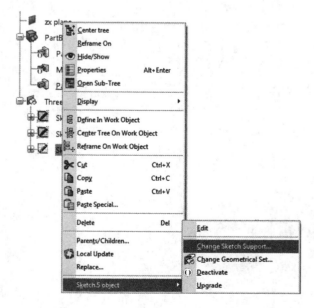

In the resulting dialogue box, for the "Planar Support Type," select the top face of the base. Close the dialogue box by choosing "OK."

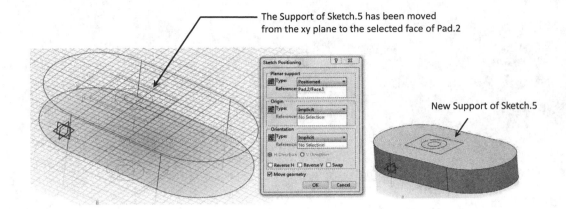

The Support of Sketch.5 has been moved from the xy plane to the selected face of Pad.2

New Support of Sketch.5

Select the "Pocket" icon followed by Sketch.5 as the support. The result is shown below.

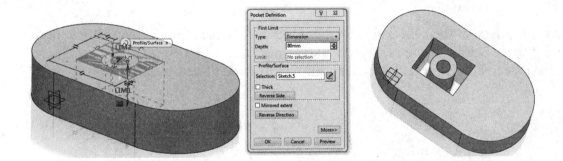

This may or may not be what you are looking for. To look into the multi pocket feature, "Deactivate" this pocket.

Next select the "Multi Pocket" icon followed by Sketch.5 as the "Support." This leads to a familiar dialogue box shown on the right.

The three curves listed in the dialogue box correspond to the two circles and the rectangle.

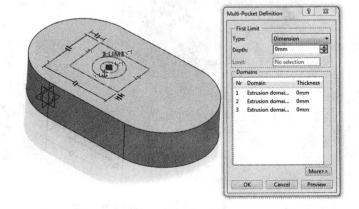

Selecting the three curves one by one and choosing appropriate pocket depth, the following part is generated.

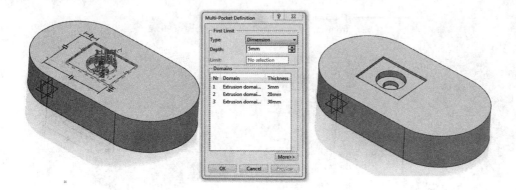

This was a summary of the multi pad and multi pocket features in 3DEXPERIENCE.

The remainder of this chapter is related to a particular feature in the ordinary pad operation. Deactivate the multi pocket just created because we will be using the base for the next discussion.

Select the top face of the base and enter the sketcher. Use the "Spline" icon 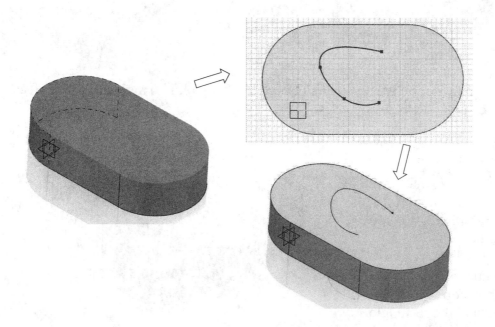 to draw a curve as shown below. There is no particular significance to the curve being a spline. It could have been any curve as long as it is an "open" curve. Finally, exit the sketcher.

Select the "Pad" icon 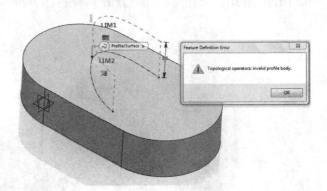 followed by choosing the sketch of the spline as the "Support." The following error window indicates that the pad operation cannot be performed. The reason behind this problem is that this spline is an "Open" curve. Open curves cannot be padded.

Press "OK" and proceed.

In the "Pad Definition" dialogue box, check "Thick" and select the "More" button.

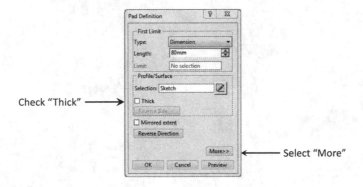

In the expanded dialogue box, input the desired "Thickness" and close the window.

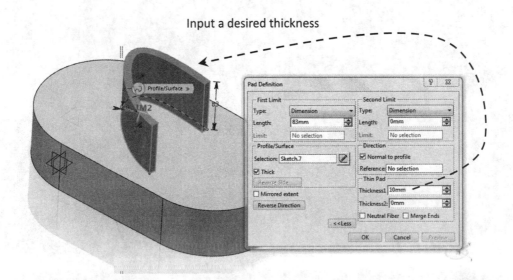

The final configuration of the part is shown below.

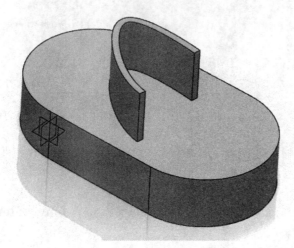

Exercise 1

In this exercise, you will be exploring the multi pad feature closer. To avoid convoluting the issue, the part to be made is quite simple. Enter the sketcher and draw five concentric circles with the radii shown below. The units (and the actual radius value) is not important.

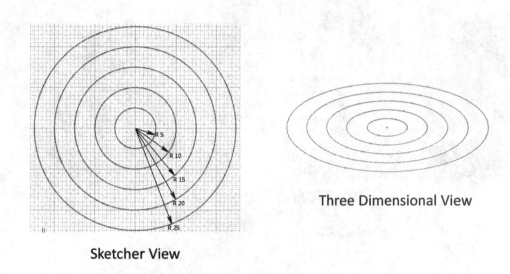

Sketcher View

Three Dimensional View

Select the "Multi-Pad" icon ![Multi-Pad] from the action bar. This leads to the dialogue box indicating the presence of five curves which have a default height of zero.

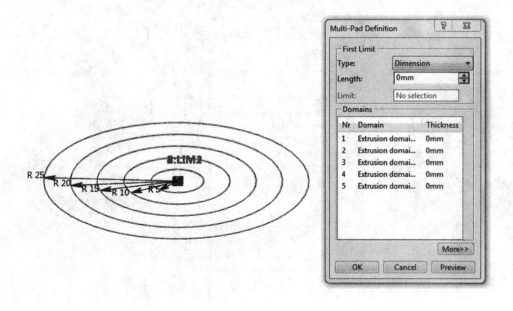

To help you understand better the mechanism behind the multi-pad functionality, we suggest that you select the following heights and observe the effect of the process.

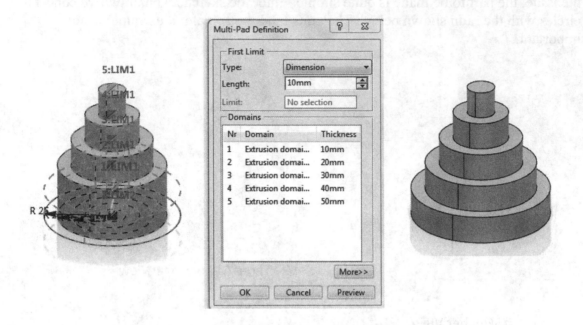

The "Length" for the largest circle is set to zero. This means it will not be padded at all.

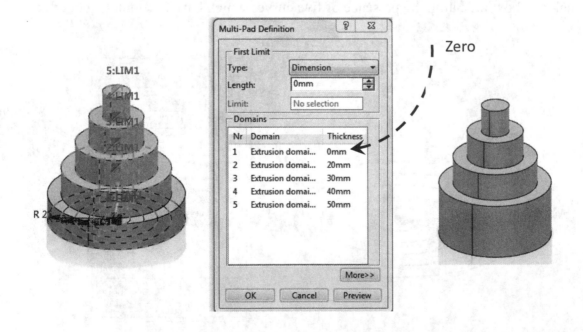

The "Length" for the largest circle is set to a negative number. This means it will be padded in the opposite direction.

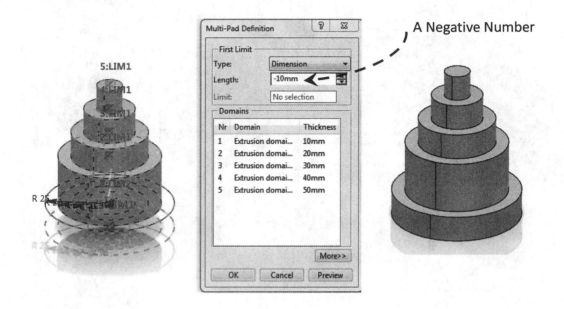

Next, change the "Length" of the second inner circle to zero. The effect is shown below.

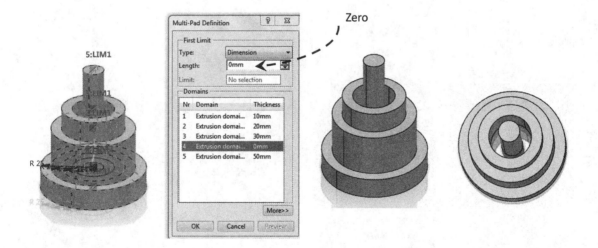

Finally, try the combination of zero and a negative number as displayed in the following figure.

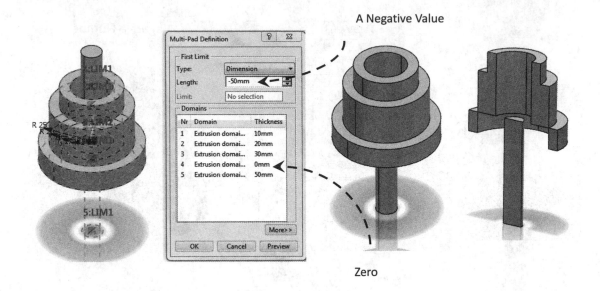

09

Measuring Items

Objective:

The purpose of this short chapter is to briefly show some functionalities of Part Design App in measuring entities in a simple CAD solid model. The part is very simple with the dimensions shown and a density of 1000 kg_m³.

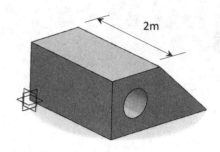

Creating the Part:

Enter the Part Design App 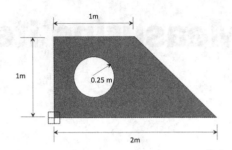 and create a part with the name of your choice. Here, the name below was used.

Nader_GEN_CH9_Physical Product00021178

Select the yz plane and enter the sketcher 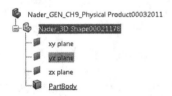.

Use the "Profile" icon to create the sketch shown with the appropriate dimensions.

Exit the sketcher and use the "Pad" icon to create the part. Use a pad length of 2m.

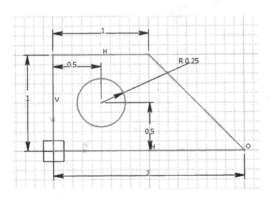

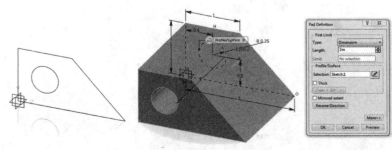

Applying Material:

Since one of the items to be measured is the inertia properties, the density of the material is needed. In order to input that, you need to apply material property to the part. Select the "Tools" tab from the bottom row of icons.

Tools tab

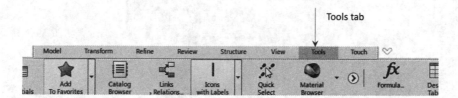

Select the "Create Material" icon  from the expanded menu.

In the dialogue box that opens, type the name of your choice for the material.

Note that this only defines a shell for the properties. The actual data has to be inputted at a later stage. The complete process for defining the material properties was described in chapter 4. Once you close the dialogue box by clicking on "OK," you will find yourself in the material database and can identify the material that you just created, namely "Measuring_Items_Gen_CH9." The database screen is shown on the next page.

Point the cursor to your material, right click, and select "Apply." You still have to return to the screen where the geometry exists and continue. This necessitates the closure of the current screen (the database screen).

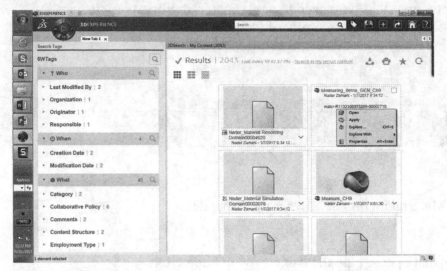

Select the "X "on the top right margin of the database screen to close the window.

You will return to the geometry window; however, the shape of the cursor is modified as shown on the right.

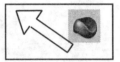

Click on "X" to close this window.

Place the cursor on the part on the screen, or on the top branch of the tree, and double click.

You will notice that the "Materials" branch is created at the very bottom of the tree as shown in the next page. You can then use the cursor to select the "Green" check mark to proceed.

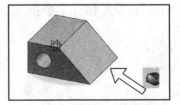

Double click on the branch of the tree immediately below the "Material" line.

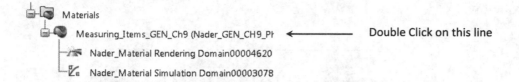

This opens up the "Edit Definition" dialogue box where you can input the density value of 1000 kg_m^3 as shown below. None of the other material properties are relevant for the measurement tools.

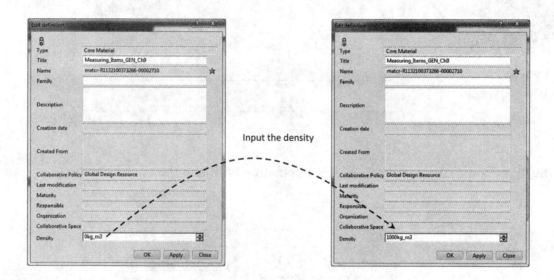

Measuring Inertia Data 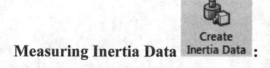 :

The measurement icons reside in the "Tools" tab of the bottom row as shown.

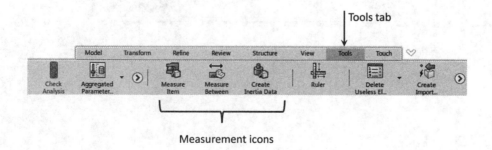

Select the "Create Inertia Data" icon 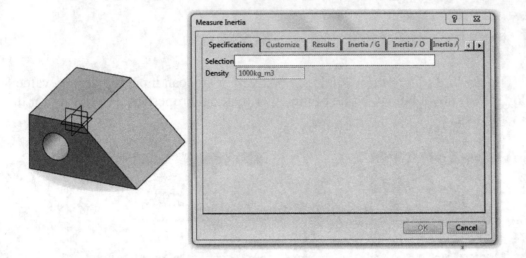. This results in the "Measure Inertia" dialogue box below.

Select the "PartBody" from the tree, which automatically fills in the "Selection box."

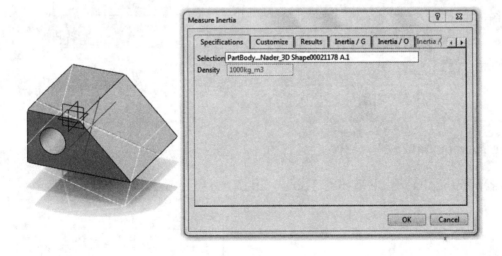

The different tabs of the dialogue box generated lead to the information displayed below.

Specification tab

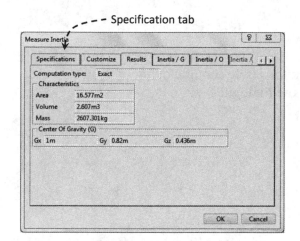

Inertia / O tab

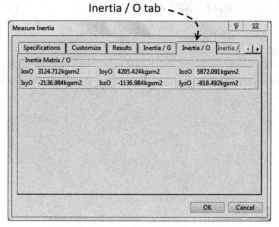

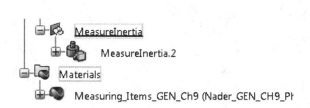

Inertia / G tab

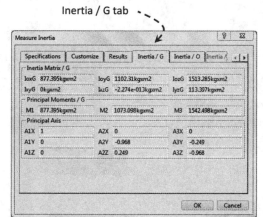

Note that every time you use one of the measurement icons, the generated information is reflected in the tree. The data can be accessed at any time by double clicking on it, and if desired, it can be deleted from the tree (right click "Delete").

Measuring Item  **:**

Select the "Measure Item" icon 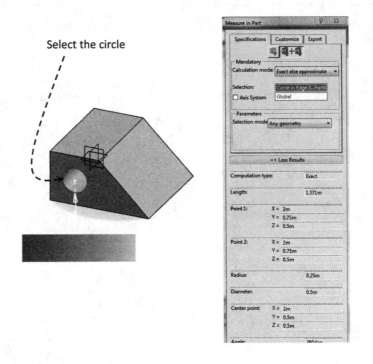 and pick the circle (not the cylinder itself).
The information on this entity is displayed in the dialogue box.

Measuring Between :

Select the "Measure Between" icon  which leads to the dialogue box on the right..

Note that it is possible to filter the geometric entities with the pull down menu for easier picks. The window below shows that only edges are being picked.

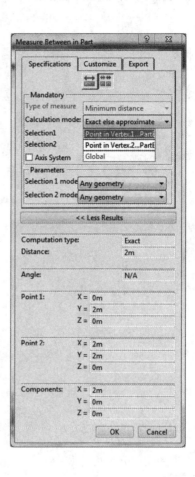

Now that the edges are filtered, select the two edges as shown, and the dialogue box displays the angle between the two edges.

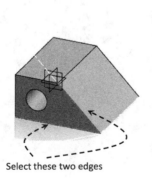

Select these two edges

As more measurements are being made, they
clutter the tree. These can be deleted at any time.
For example, select the three measurements
shown, right click and choose "Delete."

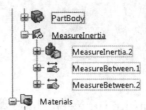

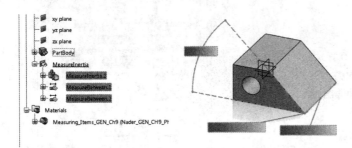

Parametrizing a Solid Model

Objective:

While the focus of this textbook is on the "Essentials of CAD Modeling in 3DEXPERIENCE," the author feels that the subject of parametric modeling, given its potential to significantly improve design times in digital product creation activities, warrants a brief discussion to introduce the topic to those readers not already familiar with it.

In the context of mechanism design, there are tremendous opportunities to take advantage of parametric design. As one example, consider the design of a typical piston engine. As digital design tools continue to mature, more and more analytical models are driving the design and development process. The outputs of those models often relate to the key geometric parameters of the design. In the engine case, these outputs may include things like bore, stroke, vee angle, compression ratio, etc. An organization that can develop a parametric CAD model of an engine can easily, quickly, and accurately update the model as key parameters change.

To explain the concept, consider the hammer which was modeled in chapter 2. The plan is to parametrize this solid model so that there are 3 independent parameters driving the model. These independent parameters are H, Rh, and Alfa.

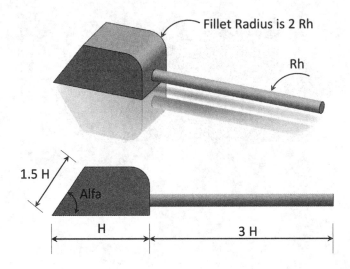

Note that the pad length of the hammer head is not specified and is assumed to have a constant value 50 mm.

Creating the Hammer with Nominal Dimensions:

The first step is to create the hammer (the part) with nominal dimensions.

Enter the Part Design App 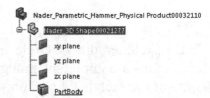 and create a part with the name of your choice. Here, the name below was used.

Nader_Parametric_Hammer_Physical Product00032110

Select the yz plane from the tree or the screen and select the "Positioned Sketch" icon

![Positioned Sketch icon] from the action bar. Create the profile shown and dimension it as indicated (mm). Note that the dimensions created correspond to the parameters defined in the previous page. Exit the sketcher and pad the profile by a nominal value of 50 mm.

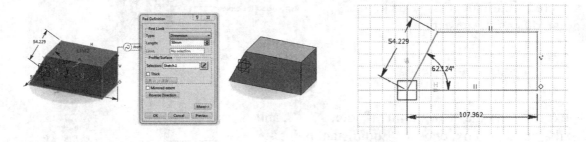

Select the "Structure" tab from the action bar. This is where the "Edge Fillet" lies.

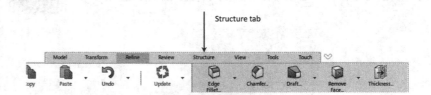

Choose the "Edge Fillet"

icon ![Edge Fillet icon] and the indicated edge. For the "Radius" use a nominal value of 15 mm.

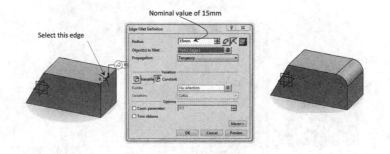

Select the end rectangular face of the hammer and
enter the sketcher.

Select this rectangular flat face
and enter the sketcher

In the sketcher, draw a circle and center it. These kinds of
operations are important enough to warrant repetition, in
spite of the fact that it was presented in chapter 2.

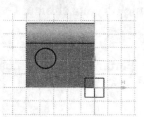

In order to center the circle vertically
make the selections 1,2,3 in the
indicated order. These have to be
selected simultaneously (Ctrl key
down during the selection).

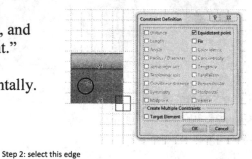

Step 1: select this edge

Step 3: select the center

Step 2: select this edge

Next, click on the "Constraint…" icon   , and
in the dialogue box, choose "Equidistant point."

Repeat the process to center the circle horizontally.

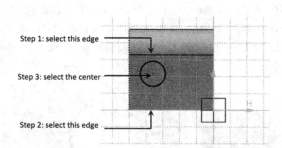

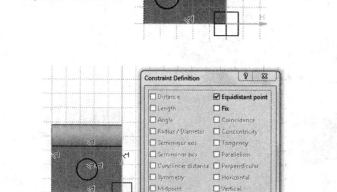

Step 1: select this edge

Step 3: select the center

Step 2: select this edge

Make sure to dimension the circle as it is one of the parameters driving the model.

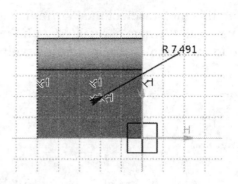

Exit the sketcher and pad the circle by a nominal value of 200 mm.

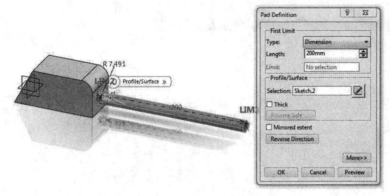

f(x) icon :

Although there are six variables involved in this part, only three of them are independent of each other: namely, Rh, Alfa, H. Therefore, only three variables need to be defined. Two are of the "Length" type, and one "Angle" type.

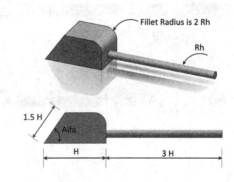

Select the Tools tab from the bottom row.

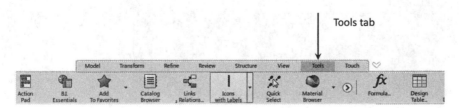

From this menu, select the "Formula" icon 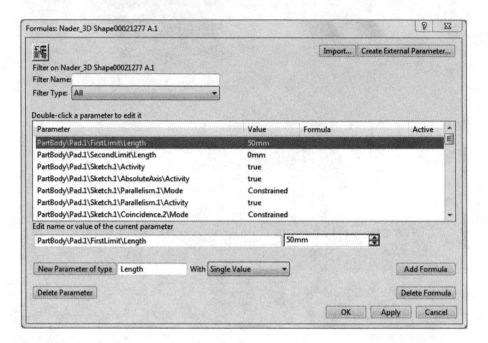. This opens a major dialogue box which contains all the data associated with the part under study. Every single entity that has a role in the hammer can be located within this window.

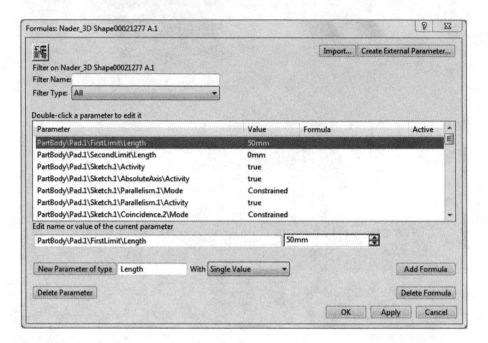

Note that by selecting different branches of the "PartBody," the different entities associated with that selection appear in the window. For example, if "Edge Fillet.1" is selected, the window appears as shown below.

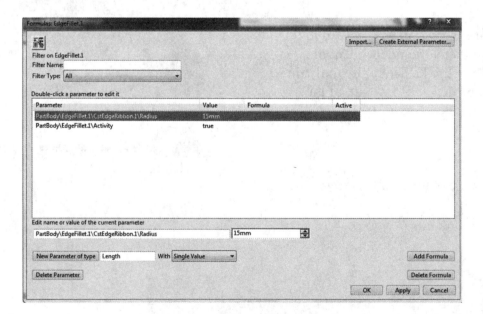

Pick "Pad.2" from the tree and the window displays only the entities associated with Pad.2.

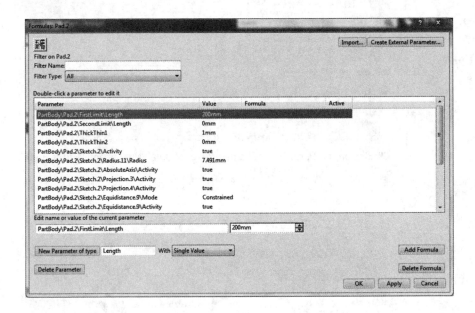

For the remainder of the chapter, select the top level branch of the tree so that all entities are shown.

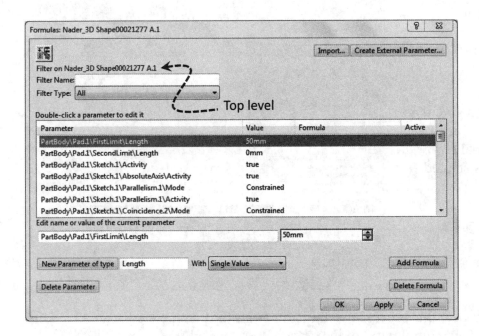

Any values can be changed from within this dialogue box

Creating Parameters:

Concentrate on the
bottom left corner of the
"Formulas" window
from the previous page.
The zoomed area is
shown below.

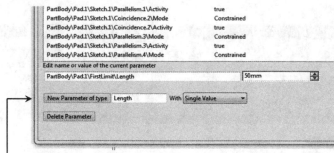

Clicking on this button creates a parameter of default name and type "Length"

Click on the button "New
Parameter of Type"; this
will immediately try to
create a parameter with the
name "Length.1."

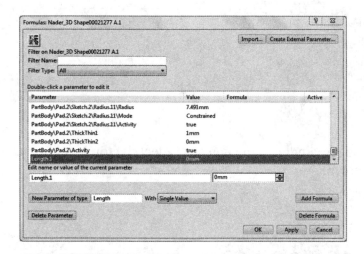

Change the name of the
parameter to H and give it a
value of 107 mm which is
roughly the nominal size
when the part was created.

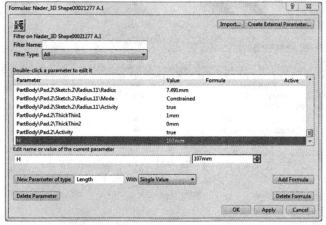

You will have to repeat this process two more times for the parameters Rh an Alfa. Due
to the importance (and complexity) of the process these are fully presented.

Click on the button "New Parameter of Type"; this will immediately try to create a parameter with the name "Length.2."

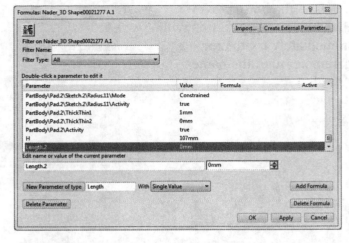

Change the name of the parameter to Rh and give it a value of 7 mm which is roughly the nominal size when the part was created.

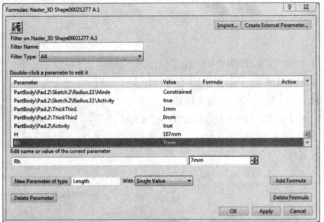

The third parameter Alfa is of type "Angle"; therefore, one first should change the type.
Place the cursor in the bottom left box which currently has type "Length." Left click and from the expanded list, select "Angle." This allows you to define the angle Alfa.

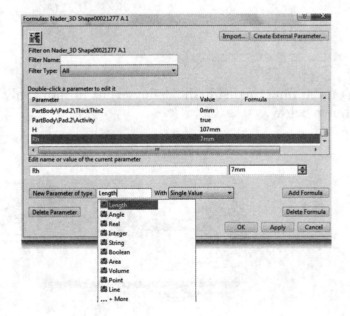

Click on the button "New Parameter of Type"; this will immediately try to create a parameter with the name "Angle.1."

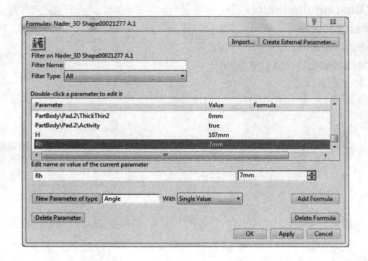

Change the name of the parameter to Alfa and give it a value of 62 deg which is roughly the nominal size when the part was created.

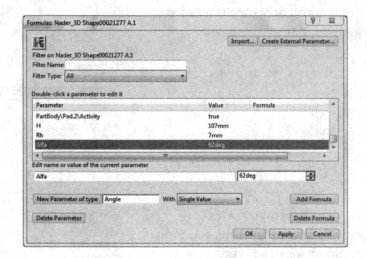

You can filter the list in the dialogue box to show only the renamed created parameters as shown below.

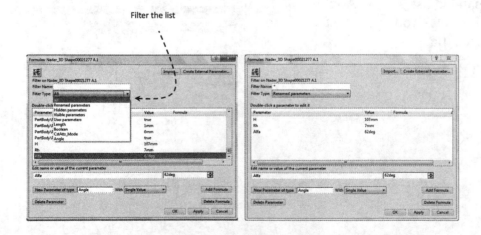

Note that these parameters have been created and were assigned values; however, they are not associated with the geometry of the hammer yet. The values of these parameters can be changed from the current dialogue box. These parameters can also be conveniently displayed in the tree for quick access.

The Procedure for Displaying the Parameters and Formulas in the Tree:

From the top right corner of the screen, shown below, select the "Me" icon followed by "Preferences." This results in the "Preferences" dialogue box opening, shown on the next page. The Catia v5 users may recognize this as the "Options" dialogue box where all the settings were accessible.

This has exactly the same functionalities. Any desired deviations from the default settings in 3DEXPERIENCE have to be initiated through this window.

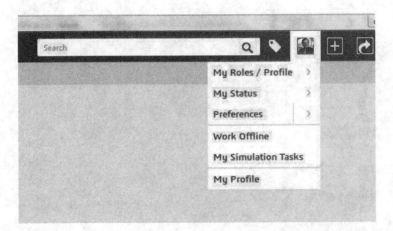

Navigate the tree in the left margin of the dialogue box and select "3D Shape Infrastructure" branch.

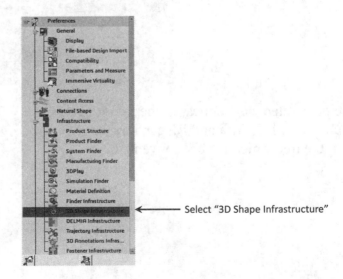

Note that there are no
check boxes next to:

Constraints
Parameters
Relations

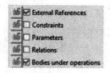

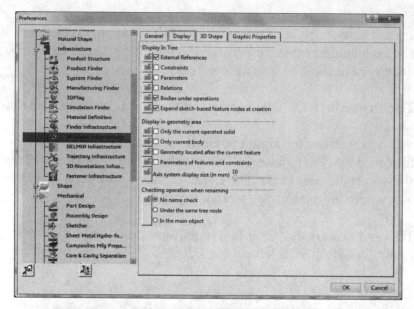

Check these three boxes
and press "OK."

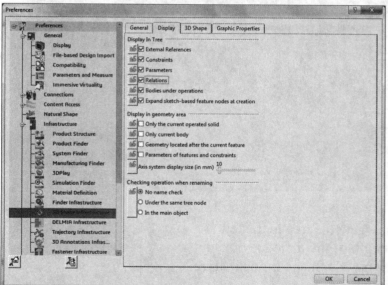

The parameters now appear in the tree structure.
The values of H, Alfa and Rh can now be changed
from the tree which is very convenient.

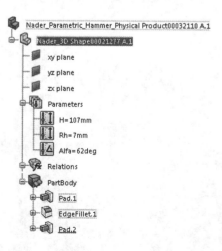

Relating the Parameters H, Rh and Alfa to the CAD Model:

Select the "Formula" icon 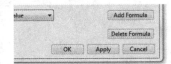 from the bottom row. This opens the major dialogue box conntaining all the data including the parameters created. If you click on the hammer head on the tree, only the data for the hammer head is kept and only dimensions associated with the hammer head are displayed on the screen.

From the screen select the dimension shown below. The database name associated with this dimension is immediately identified. Recall that this dimension is 1.5H.

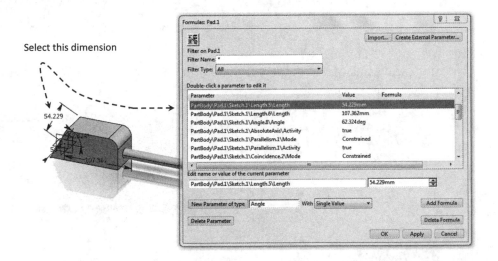

Press the "Add Formula" button at the bottom right margin of the dialogue box.

This lands you in the "Formula Editor" box where formulas can be inputted. In the empty box you need to type 1.5*H. In the event that you do not recall the name of the existing parameters, from the middle column select "Renamed Parameters."

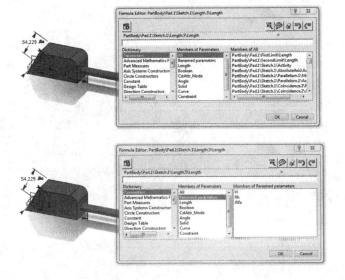

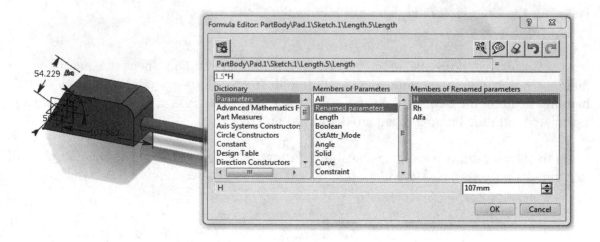

Type the formula and click "OK." This will land you back in the "Formulas" window.

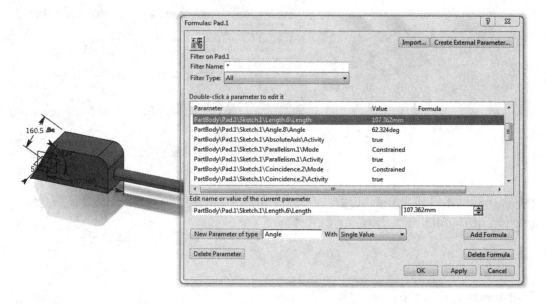

From the screen select the angle dimension shown below. The database name associated with this dimension is immediately identified. Recall that this dimension is equal to Alfa.

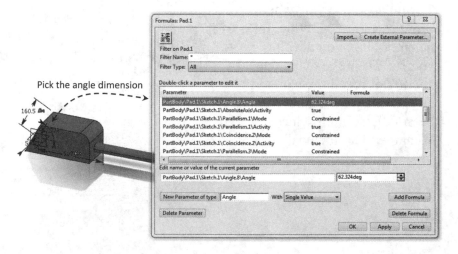

Press the "Add Formula" button at the bottom right margin of the dialogue box.

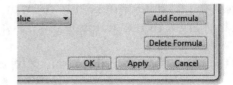

In the blank formula place holder type "Alfa."

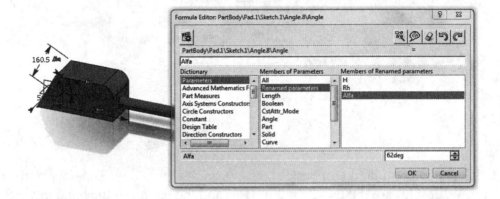

Click on "OK" to land you back in the "Formulas" window. We need to input the formula Rf = 2 Rh; however, Rf is not in Pad.1 (which is the hammer head). From the screen pick the fillet that was created. This will change the contents of the window and you will only see the entities pertaining to the edge fillet. See below.

From the screen, select the fillet radius dimension shown below. The database name associated with this dimension is immediately identified.

Select the edge fillet

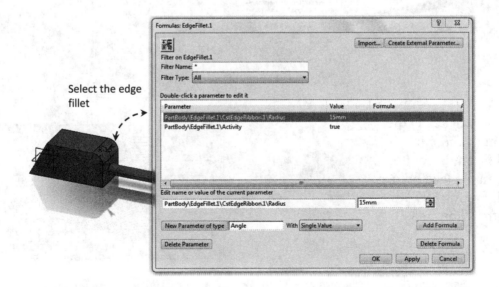

Press the "Add Formula" button at the bottom right margin of the dialogue box.

In the blank formula place holder type 2*Rh.

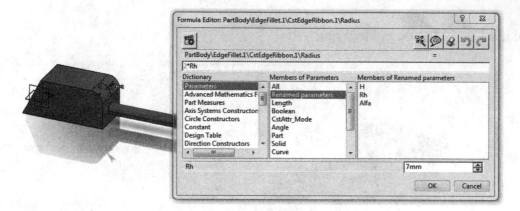

Click on "OK" to land you back in the "Formulas" window. The only remaining entities to be dealt with are the handle radius (Rh) and the length of the handle which is to be 3H. However, both of these entities are in Pad.2. Therefore, select the hammer handle by clicking on it in the screen. The contents of the "Formulas" window changes.

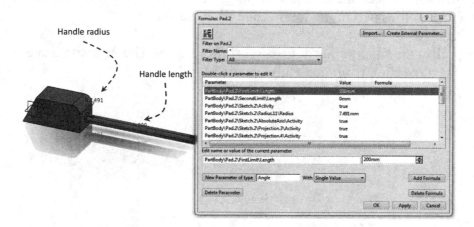

From the screen select the handle length and click on the "Add Formula" button. In the formula place holder, type 3*H. Press " OK" to return to the "Formulas" window.

From the screen select the handle radius and click on the "Add Formula" button.
In the formula place holder, type Rh. Press " OK" to return to the "Formulas" window.

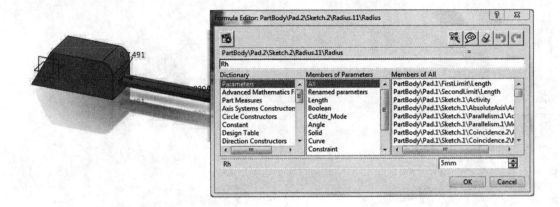

At this point, we have defined all parameters and all relationships that tie them with the geometry of the hammer. All parameters and formulas are showing on the tree also.

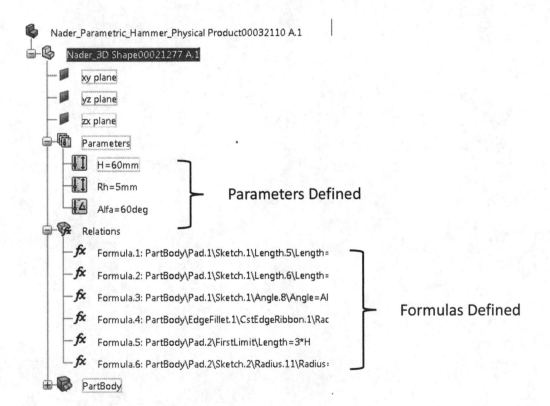

By changing the parameters H, Rh, and Alfa, the shape of the hammer changes. Here are some sets of parameters and the associated shapes.

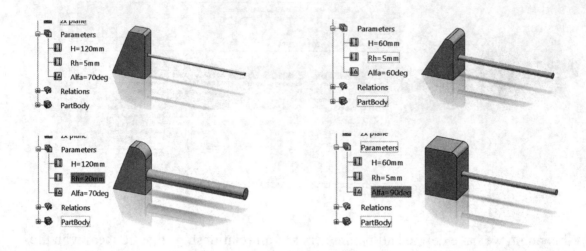

Exercise 1:

Consider the part shown below. Use the driving parameters RTOP, RSIDE, ALFA, R1, R2, and L to parametrize the solid model. Make sure that the center of the two circles always remain centered on their supports.

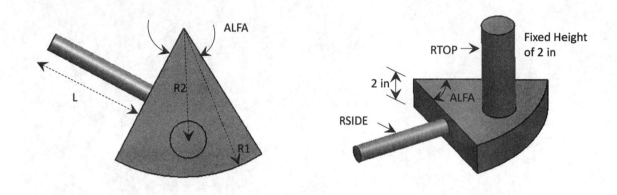

Exercise 2:

Consider the part shown below. Use the driving parameters RSIDE, RTOP, ALFA, BETA, B and L to parametrize the solid model. Make sure that the center of the two circles always remain centered on their supports.

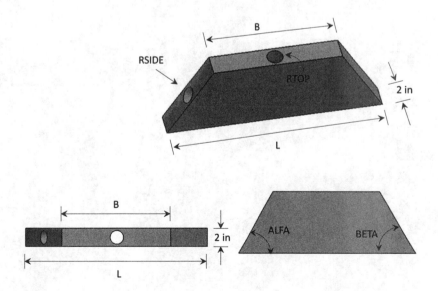

NOTES:

Design Table

Objective:

Earlier in this book, a parametric model of a hammer was made. This parametric model was driven by three independent parameters, H, Rh, and Alfa. The user can change these values at will, and the hammer will be updated. Imagine that a company manufactures such hammers in specific dimensions. That being the case, there is no reason for anyone to change these parameters arbitrarily. It makes more sense that a database of available dimensions is created and used. This process is referred to as making a "Design Table."

In this chapter, the process of creating a design table is explained. It is a very powerful tool that can be effectively used by the reader. The hammer is shown below where there are three independent parameters (H, Rh, Alfa) and three explicit relationships (1.5H, 2Rh, and 3H).

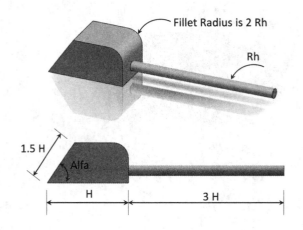
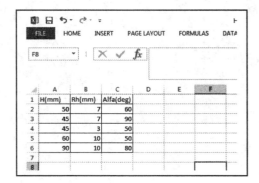

Note that the pad length of the hammer head is not specified and will be assumed to be a constant of 50 mm.

Design Table Approach:

By a Design table, we are referring to a database, such as an Excel spreadsheet, which contains the information for the part. Each row (or column) of the spreadsheet is associated with a particular part configuration. There are two approaches in utilizing the design table. One is to have a pre-existing spreadsheet at the outset, and the second approach is to create the spreadsheet as the part is being generated. We choose to follow the latter approach. This entails creating a hammer with nominal dimensions first. Therefore, the first few pages are a repetition of the material in chapter 2 and chapter 10.

Creating the Hammer with Nominal Dimensions:

The first step is to create the hammer (the part) with nominal dimensions.

Enter the Part Design App  and create a part with the name of your choice. Here, the name below was used.

Nader_Design_Table_Physical Product00032755

Pick the yz plane from the tree or the screen and select the "Positioned Sketch" icon from the bottom row menu (i.e., the action bar). Create the profile shown and dimension it as indicated (mm). Note that the dimensions created correspond to the parameters defined in the previous page. Exit the sketcher and pad the profile by a nominal value of 50 mm.

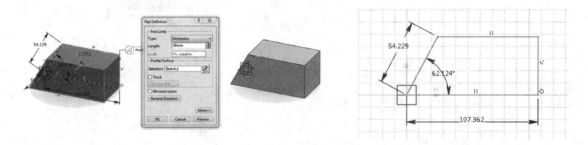

Select the "Refine" tab from the row of icons at the bottom of the screen. This is where the "Edge Fillet" lies.

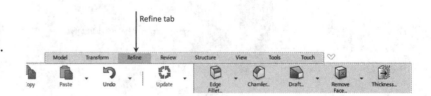

Select the "Edge Fillet" icon 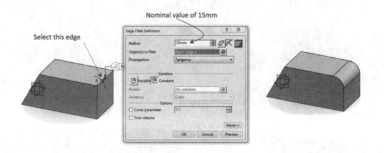 and the indicated edge. For the "Radius" use a nominal value of 15 mm.

Select the end rectangular face of the hammer and
enter the sketcher.

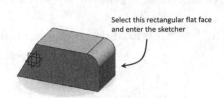

Select this rectangular flat face
and enter the sketcher

In the sketcher, draw a circle and center it. These kind of
operations are important enough to warrant repetition.

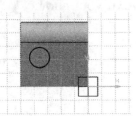

In order to center the circle vertically,
make the selections 1,2,3 in the
indicated order. These have to be
selected simultaneously (Ctrl key
down during selection).

Step 1: select this edge

Step 3: select the center

Step 2: select this edge

Next, click on the "Constraint…" icon 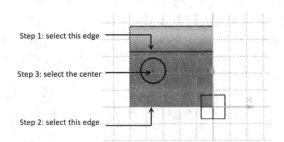, and
in the dialogue box choose "Equidistant point."

Repeat the process to center the circle horizontally.

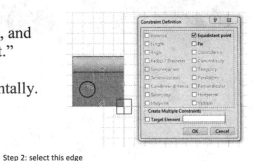

Step 1: select this edge

Step 3: select the center

Step 2: select this edge

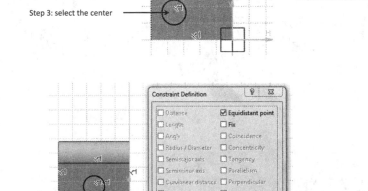

Dimension the circle as it is one of the parameters driving the model.

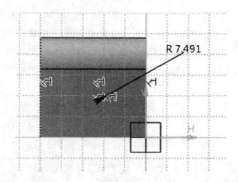

R 7.491

Exit the sketcher and pad the circle by a nominal value of 200 mm.

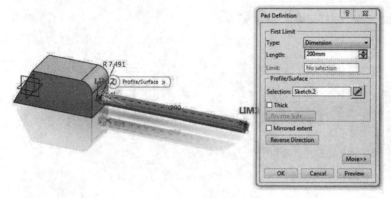

f(x) icon Formula :

Although there are six variables involved in this part, only three of them are independent of each other. namely, Rh, Alfa, H. Therefore, only three variables need to be defined. Two are of the "Length" type, and one "Angle" type.

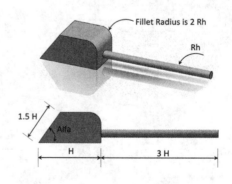

Fillet Radius is 2 Rh

Rh

1.5 H

Alfa

H   3 H

Select the Tools tab from the bottom row.

Tools tab

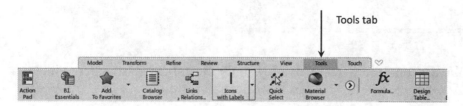

From this menu, select the "Formula" icon . This opens a major dialogue box which contains all the data associated with the part under study. Every single entity that has a role in the hammer can be located within this window.

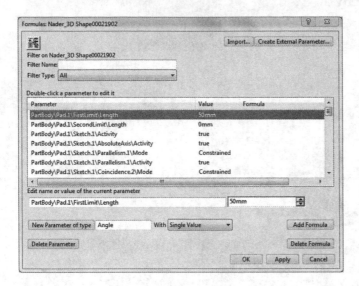

Note that by selecting different branches of the "PartBody," the different entities associated with that selection appear in the window. For example, if "Edge Fillet.1" is selected, the window appears as shown below.

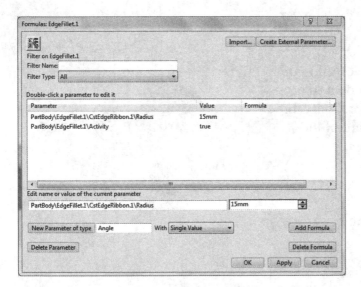

Pick "Pad.2" from the tree and the window displays only the entities associated with Pad.2.

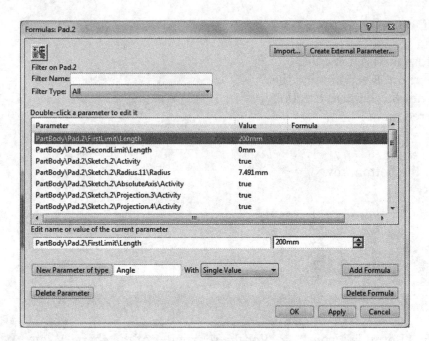

For the remainder of the chapter, select the top level of the tree so that all entities are shown.

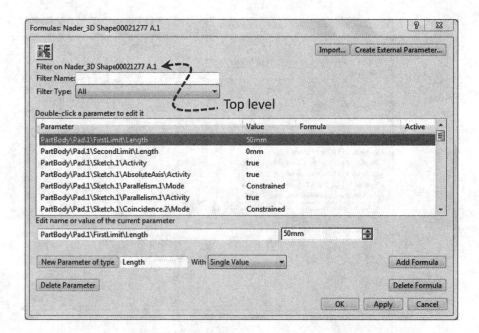

Any values can be changed from within this dialogue box.

Renaming Some of the Dimensions:

The first step in this process is to rename the
dimensions shown on the right. Keep in mind that
renaming a dimension is not the same as creating
a parameter with the desired name.

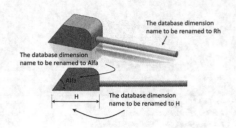

Select the Tools tab from the bottom row.

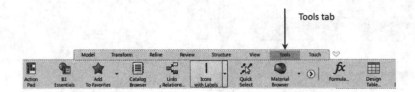

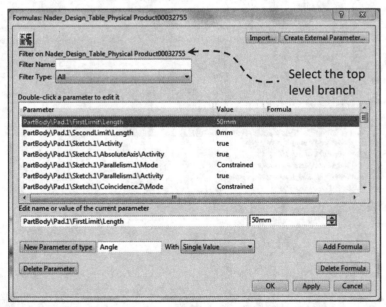

From this menu, select the "Formula" icon ![fx Formula]. For the remainder of the chapter, select
the top level of the tree so that all entities are shown. Once you click on the part (on the
screen), all the dimensions associated with the model appear on the screen.

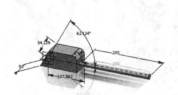

Using the cursor, from the screen, select the angle dimension. The software immediately
locates the database name of that dimension and displays it in the window. The software
shows that the default name of this dimension is
PartBody\Pad.1\Sletch.1\Angle.8\Angle.

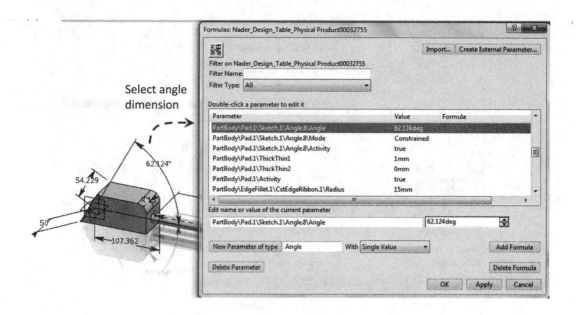

Retype a new name for this dimension; use Alfa as the new name.

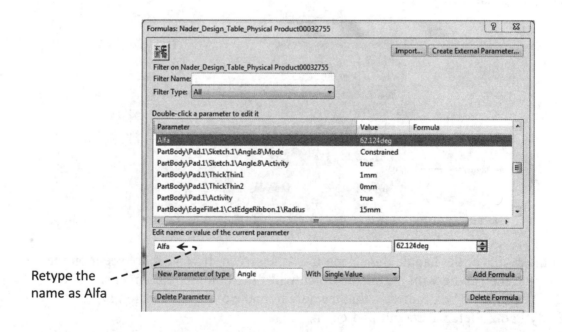

Next, select the horizontal dimension of the hammer head from the sketcher. The dialogue box indicates that the default name of this dimension is PartBody\Pad.1\Sletch.1\Length.5\Length.

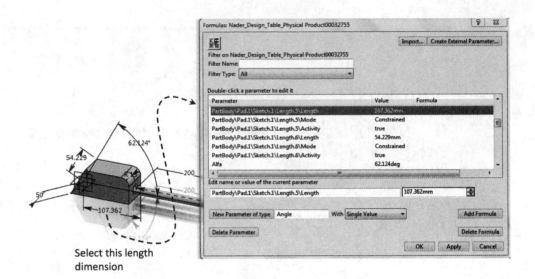

Select this length
dimension

Retype a new name for this dimension; use H as the new name.

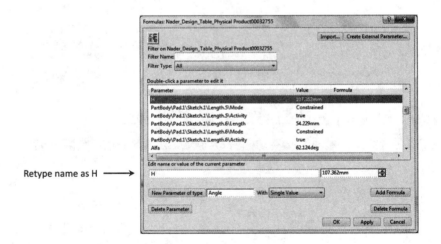

Retype name as H ⟶

Select the radius of the handle dimension from the screen. If you cannot see it on the screen, pick the handle with the cursor which will filter out only the dimensions for Pad.2. The dialogue box indicates that the default name of this dimension is PartBody\Pad.2\Sletch.2\Length.11\Length.

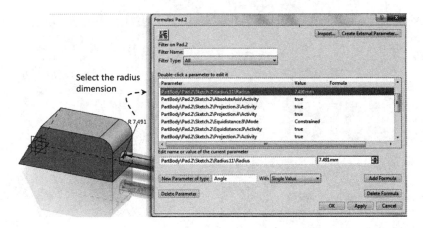

Select the radius
dimension

Change the name to Rh.

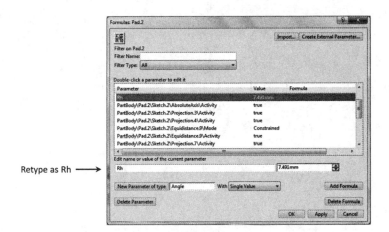

Retype as Rh ⟶

At this point, you have renamed three dimensions to Alfa, H and Rh. Once again, keep in mind that renaming entities is not the same as creating parameters. To see these renamed dimensions only, select the top level branch of the tree, and using the pulldown menu, as the "Filter Type" select "Renamed Parameters."

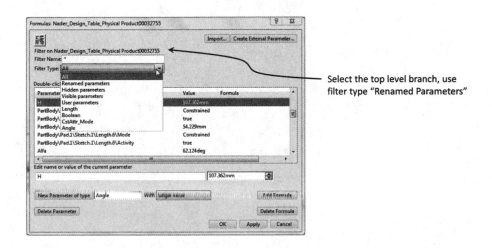

Select the top level branch, use
filter type "Renamed Parameters"

This results in the window showing only the renamed parameters.

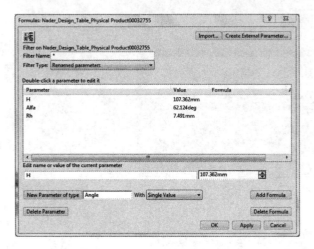

Creating the Equations:

The next task is to create the equations (formulas) dealing with the "1.5*H," "2*Rh," and "3*H." To make this easier, select the top level branch of the tree so that the entire database information appears in the "Formulas" dialogue box.

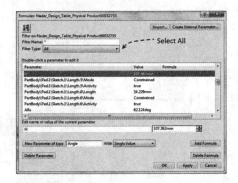

Click on the part (on the screen) so that all the dimensions are displayed. Select the dimension of the slanted side of the hammer head shown. The software locates the actual name for this dimension in the database. The name of this dimension is PartBody\Pad.1\Sketch.1\Length.6\Length.

Select this dimension; add a formula = 1.5*H

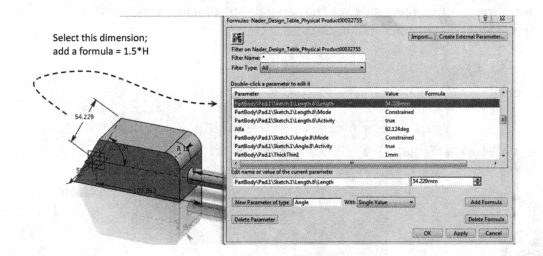

Select the "Add Formula" button on the bottom right margin of the dialogue box shown in the image above.

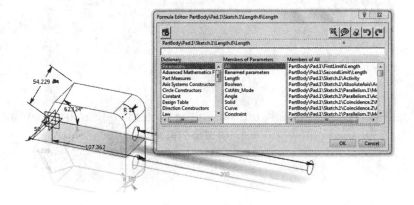

In the "Formulas Editor" dialogue box, complete the equation by typing "1.5*H."

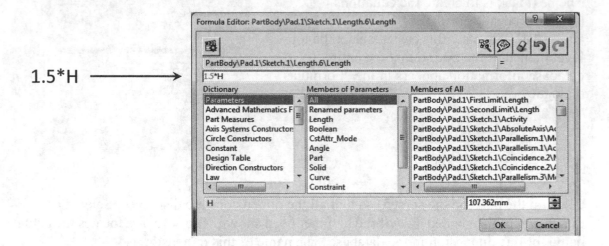

Select the radius dimension of the fillet edge shown. The software locates the actual name for this dimension in the database. The name of this dimension is PartBody\EdgeFillet.1\CstEdgeRibbon.1\Radius.

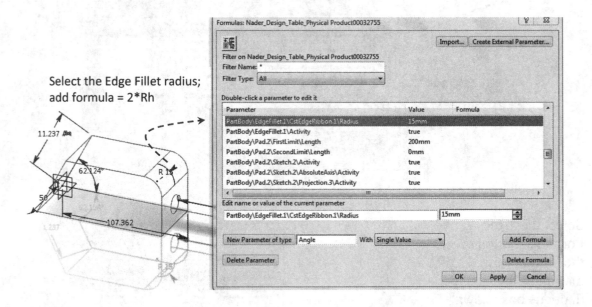

Select the 'Add Formula" button on the bottom right margin of the dialogue box shown earlier. For the right-hand side of the equation, type "2*Rh."

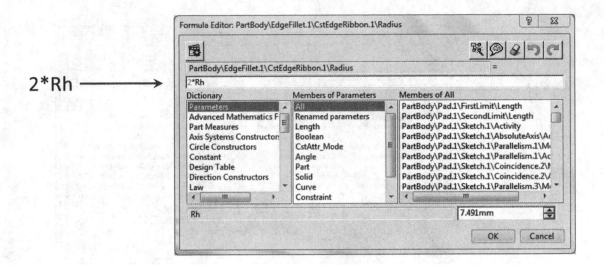

2*Rh

Select the pad dimension of the handle as shown. The software locates the actual name for this dimension in the database. The name of this dimension is PartBody\Pad.2\FirstLimit\Length.

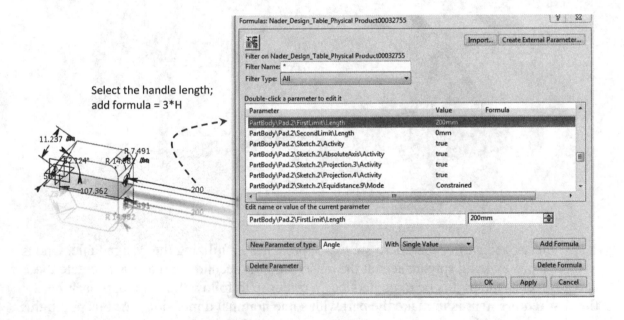

Select the "Add Formula" button on the bottom right margin of the dialogue box shown earlier. For the right-hand side of the equation, type "3*H."

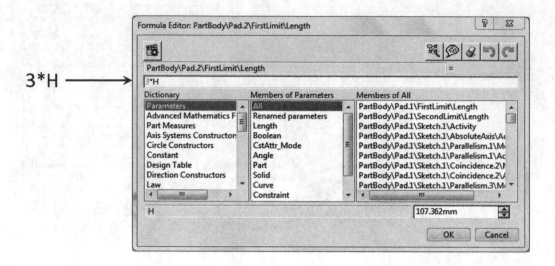

3*H

Select "OK" to return to the "Formulas" dialogue box and "Ok" one more time to return to the 3D space. The hammer will be updated according to the nominal dimensions while respecting the formulas supplied. The shape of the hammer gets displayed on the screen.

It was mentioned earlier that there are two approaches in utilizing the design table. One is to have a pre-existing spreadsheet at the outset, and the second approach is to create the spreadsheet as the part is being generated. We choose to follow the latter approach but the first requirement is to make the part with some nominal dimensions. At this point, this task has been accomplished.

Design Table Creation:

Make sure that you are in the "Tools" tab.

Tools tab

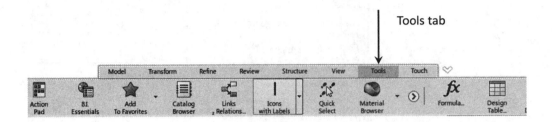

Select the "Design Table" icon 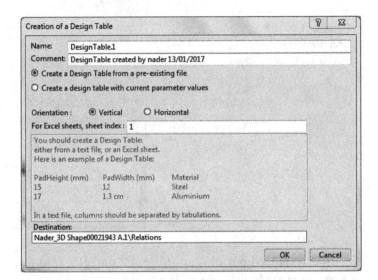 which leads to the dialogue box shown on the right. Notice that there are two "Radio" buttons. You need to select the **second button**.

Select the second radio button

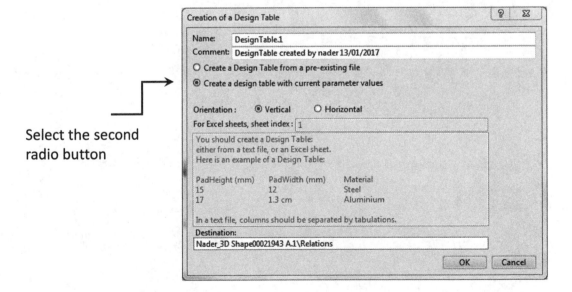

Select "OK."

In the resulting dialogue box, use the pulldown menu to filter out everything except the "Renamed Parameters" as shown.

Filter out so that
only Renamed
Parameters are shown

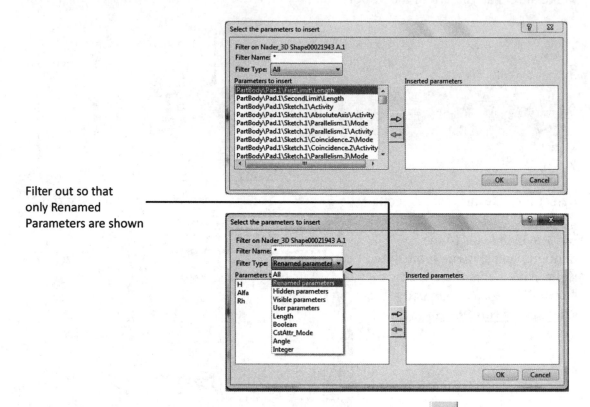

Select the renamed parameters H, Alfa, and Rh, and use the arrow button to send them to the right hand side of the table.

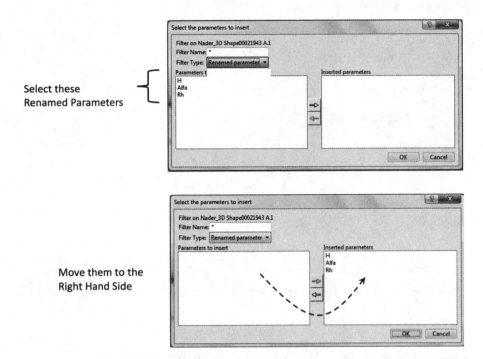

Select these
Renamed Parameters

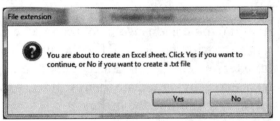

Move them to the
Right Hand Side

Upon clicking on "OK," you are reminded that an Excel file is about to be created. Select "YES."

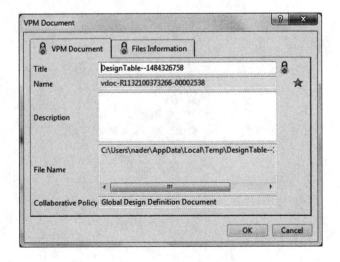

Select "OK" for the next dialogue box.

A design table has been generated as the box "DesignTable.1" indicates. The nominal dimensions have been used for this purpose.

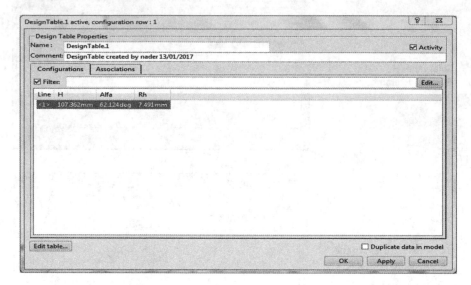

This window has two tabs, "Configuration" and "Association." Selecting the "Association" tab, the window reveals the following information.

In the event that the dimensions were not renamed earlier, one would first have to create three true parameters with the names H, Alfa, and Rh. The middle column would have these three parameters listed. The next step would be to go through the screen, and select the dimensions needed, and associate them with H, Alfa, and Rh manually. Note that renaming considerably simplified the process.

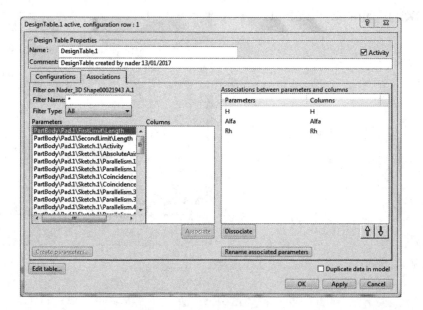

Clicking the button "Edit table," in the bottom left margin of the above dialogue box, opens the editable Excel spreadsheet.

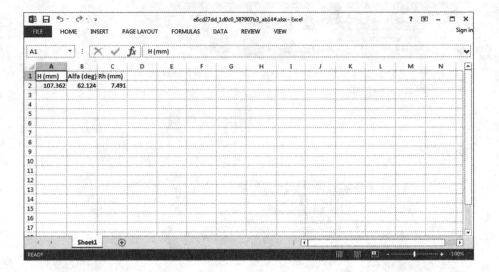

Notice that the nominal dimensions appear in the second row (below the headings). If desired, this row can be completely deleted and new entries be added. We have chosen to edit the spreadsheet to have the entries below.

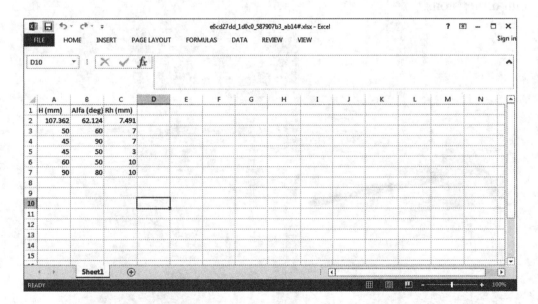

In order to proceed further, you have to save this spreadsheet 🖫 **and then "Close" it by clicking on** ✕ **on the upper right margin.**

Upon closing the spreadsheet, the following dialogue box appears. Accept it by selecting "Close."

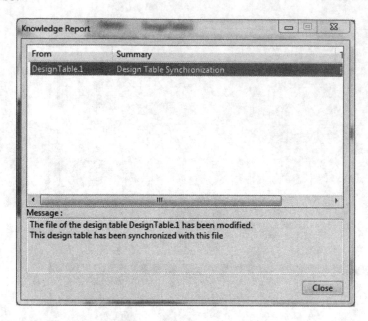

Selecting the configuration tab indicates that the Excel spreadsheet has been linked to the model. If you select the first row of the table, naturally you get the hammer with nominal dimensions.

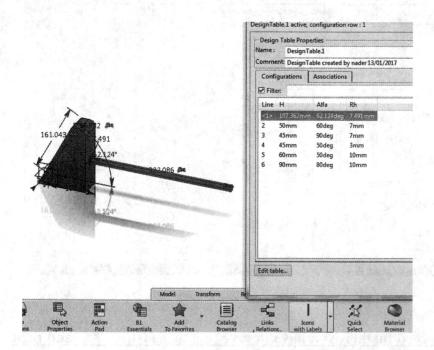

Selecting the second row generates the new geometry.

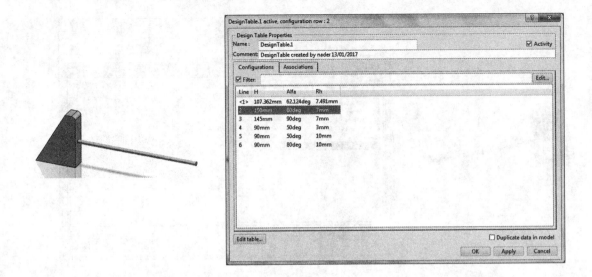

The 3rd row will give the following hammer configuration.

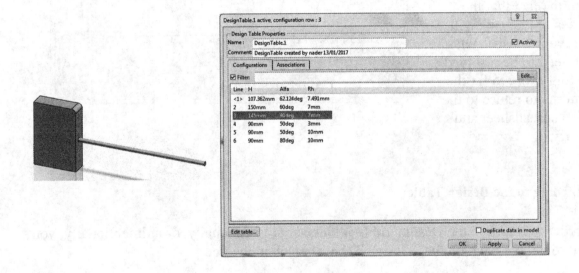

The last row produces the part shown below.

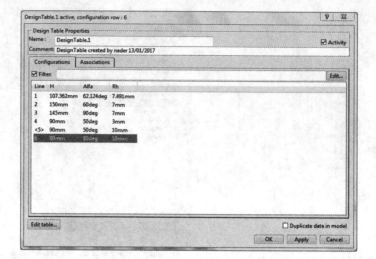

If the 4th row of the table is selected an error message appears. It stems from the fact that the entries of that row will involve inconsistencies that need to be resolved. The only way to fix the matter is to return to the Excel spreadsheet and modify it.

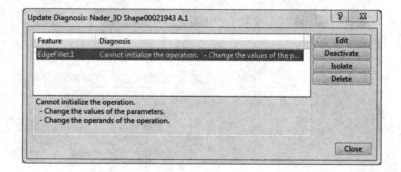

Returning to the Design Table:

In order to return to the Design Table if kicked out intentionally, or unintentionally, you need to double click on the "Design Table" branch in the tree.

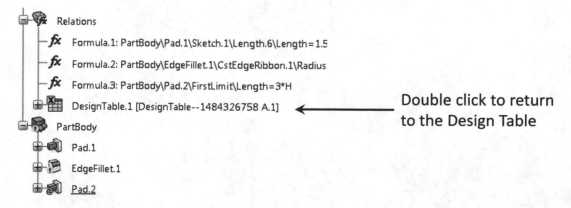

Double click to return to the Design Table

Needless to say, in order to double click on the branch, you need to be able to see it in the first place. The procedure to display this kind of information in the tree was explained on page 11 of Chapter 10. This double clicking lands you in the design table and one can proceed with further exploration.

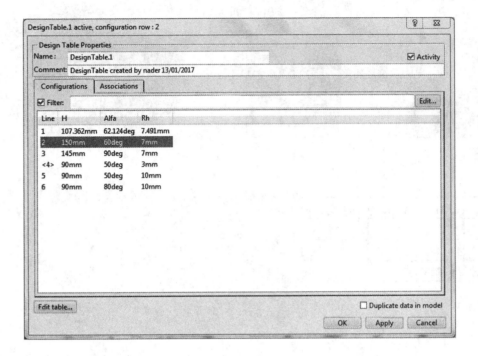

Exercise 1:

Create a design table for the following part and the values given in the table below.

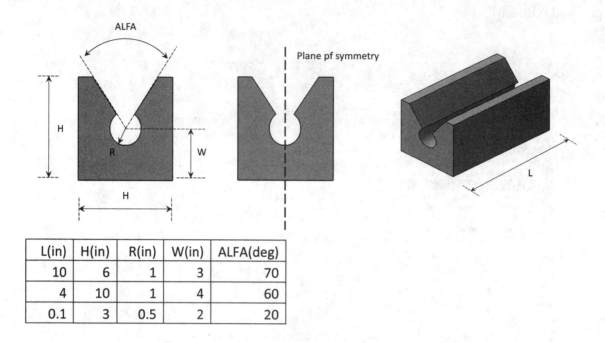

L(in)	H(in)	R(in)	W(in)	ALFA(deg)
10	6	1	3	70
4	10	1	4	60
0.1	3	0.5	2	20

Exercise 2:

Create a design table for the following part and the values given in the table below.

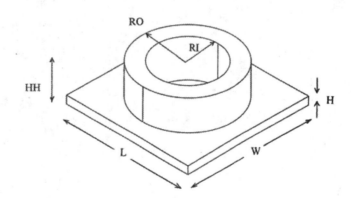

HH(in)	H(in)	RO(in)	RI(in)	L(in)	W(in)
4	0.1	1.5	0.5	3.5	10
3	1	2	1.5	8	8
2	0.5	3	2	8	20

Miscellaneous Operations, Stiffener, Helix, ThickSurface

Objective:

In this chapter, three useful operations dealing with the creation of Stiffener, Helix, and ThickSurface functionalities are discussed.

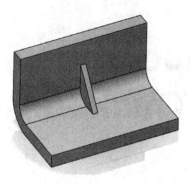

Creation of a Stiffener:

Select the yz plane and enter the sketcher . In the sketcher, create the following drawing and dimension as indicated.

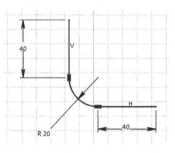

Select the entire profile (the two lines and the arc); use the "Offset" icon to get the following dialogue box.

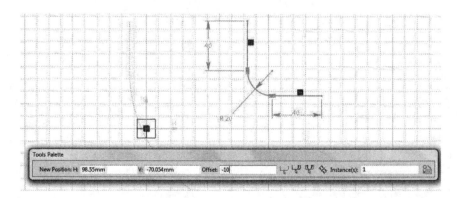

For the offset type "10mm" in the "Tools Palette." This offsets the profile by 10 mm in the direction normal to the profile as shown.

Turn the profile into a closed sketch by adding two line segments to the sketch. Make sure that the profile has no gaps.

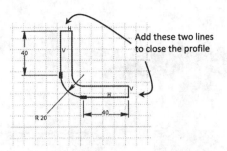

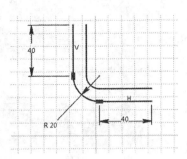

Add these two lines to close the profile

Exit the sketcher  and "Pad" the profile to create the geometry shown.

Select the "Plane" icon and create a plane which is offset from one end of the part by 50 mm.

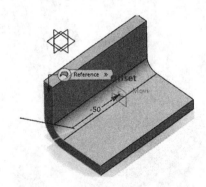

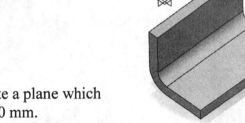

Pick this plane and enter the sketcher . In the sketcher, draw a line as shown. This line will be instrumental in creating the stiffener.

Draw this line which will become the stiffener.

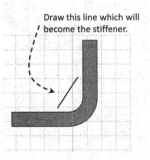

Exit the sketcher .

Select the "Stiffener" icon 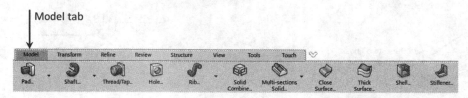 from the "Model" tab.

In the resulting dialogue box, for the "Profile" select the straight line drawn, and for the thickness input 4 mm.

The created Stiffener is shown below.

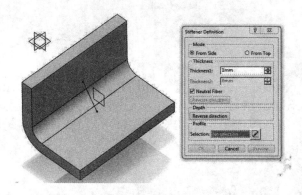

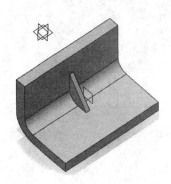

The "ThickSurface" Operation:

Use the "ThickSurface" icon 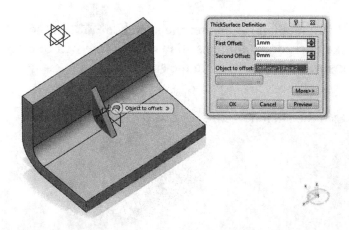 from the "Model" tab to open the following dialogue box. For the "Object to offset," select the face of the stiffener as shown. For the "First Offset" input 20 mm. You will see that the stiffener is widened by another 20 mm as if material has been added to the part.

For the final configuration, see the next page.

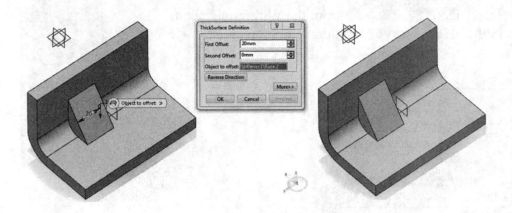

Creation of a Helix:

If you are not already in the Generative Shape Design App, you should switch to the application.

Select the "Generative Shape Design" icon to enter the App.

After landing in that App, select the "Wireframe" tab.

Wireframe tab

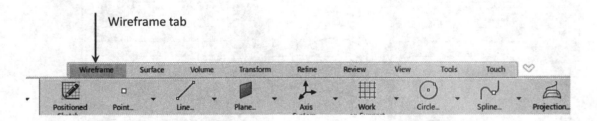

Select the "Point" icon in the Wireframe tab to create a point with coordinates (20,0,0). This point is where the helix will start.

Keep in mind that a helix has a starting point, direction, pitch and number of revolutions to be uniquely defined.

Select the "Helix" icon  from the Wireframe menu.
This results in the "Helix Curve Definition" dialogue box.

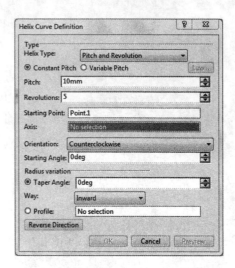

For the "Pitch" input 10 mm, for the "Starting Point" select the point (0,0,20) created earlier, and for the "Number of Revolutions" input 5. For the direction, use the pulldown menu and select the Z Axis.

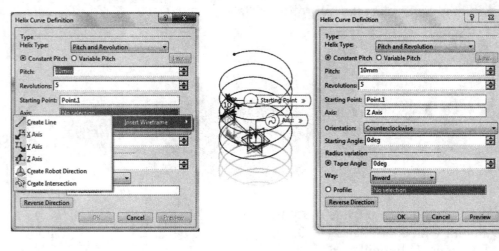

The result is the helix shown on the right.

The plan is to turn this helix into a spring.

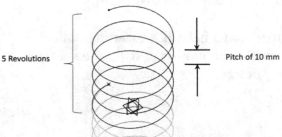

5 Revolutions

Pitch of 10 mm

Select the "Plane" icon . In the resulting dialogue box, use the pulldown menu to change the "Plane Type" to "Normal to Curve."

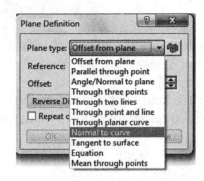

With this "Plane Type," one needs to select a curve and a point. For the "Curve" select the Helix.1, and for the "Point" select the top point of the helix. The result is shown below.

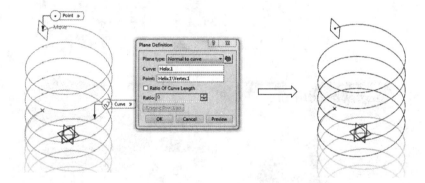

Use the "Positioned Sketch" icon 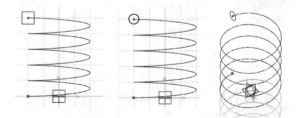 followed by the plane just constructed to enter the sketcher. In the sketcher draw a circle at the origin with roughly the size shown. Keep in mind that this circle will turn into the cross section of the spring coil. Exit the sketcher.

Select the Volume tab from the action bar (i.e., bottom row of icons).

Pick the "Volume Sweep" icon  from the menu. The "Swept Volume Definition" window pops up.

There are many options in this dialogue box, but in this introductory treatment, we use the default parameters.

For the "Profile," select the sketch which contains the circle last drawn.

For the "Guide curve," select Helix.1. This is good enough for the construction of the spring coil shown below.

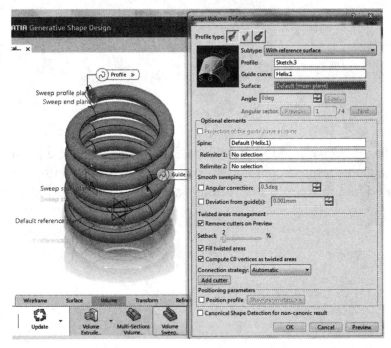

Split Operation  :

The "Split" operation appears in many applications, Part Design, Generative Shape Design, and Assembly Design to name a few.

Since the spring coil was generated in the Generative Shape Design App, we will describe the process in this application.

Select the "Split" icon  from the Transform tab.

Transform tab

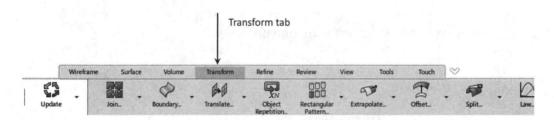

The "Split Definition" dialogue box opens. For the "Element to Cut" select the "Volume Sweep.1," for the "Cutting element" select the zx plane (from the tree or the screen). Select "OK."

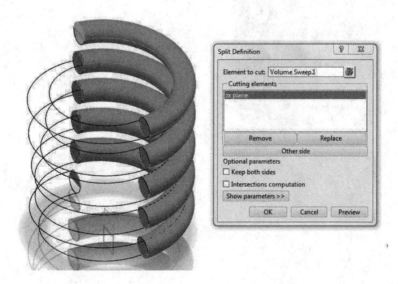

Upon pressing "OK," another window pops up.

For the next two pop-up windows, select "OK" followed by "Cancel."

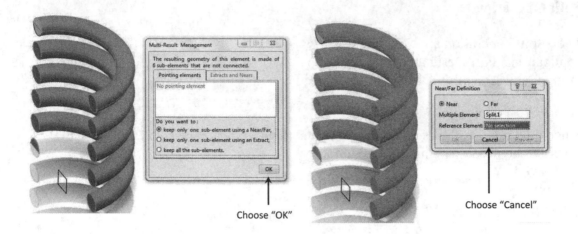

Choose "OK"   Choose "Cancel"

The final configuration of the split part is displayed below.

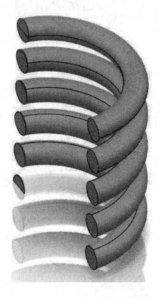

Chapter 13

Multi Section Solids

Objective:

Multi section solid is a functionality that enables the user to create complicated three dimensional objects. These solids can have twisted cross sections as shown below. One can also use the "Removed Multi Section Solids" to remove material from a part.

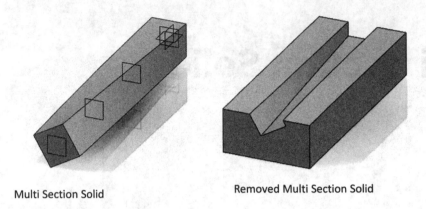

Multi Section Solid   Removed Multi Section Solid

The Sections:

Three planes will be created which are offsets of the yz plane. On the yz plane, a square is generated and on the remaining three planes, rotated squares are made. The Multi Section solid consists of these four sections.

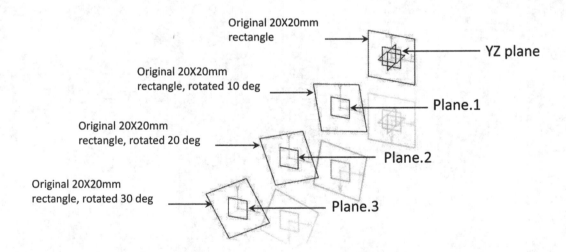

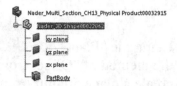

Enter the Part Design App 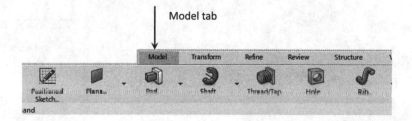 and create a part with the name of your choice. Here, the name below was used.

Nader_Multi_Section_CH13_Physical Product00032915

In order to organize the work, we create a geometric set at the outset. Select the Structure tab of the action bar.

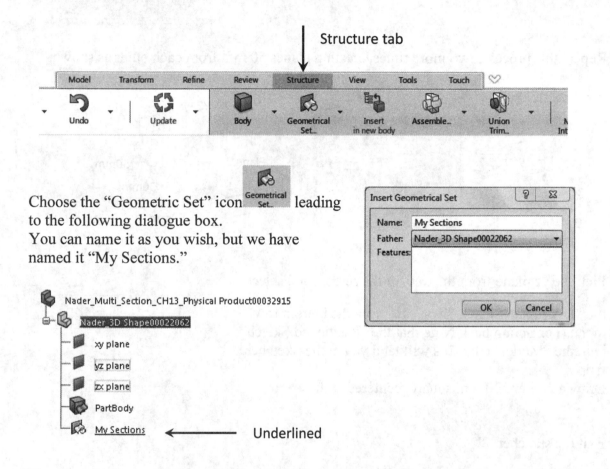

Choose the "Geometric Set" icon leading to the following dialogue box.
You can name it as you wish, but we have named it "My Sections."

Note that the geometric set "My Sections" is underlined. This means that any wireframe or surface entities that are generated will end up in this geometric set. This statement is true unless you have changed the default settings through the "Preferences" option.
In order to create the planes, select the Model tab of the action bar.

Using the "Plane" icon 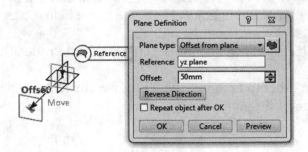 and
the method of "Offset from Plane,"
create a plane 50 mm from the YZ
plane.

Repeat this process, two more times, creating planes 50 mm from each other as shown.

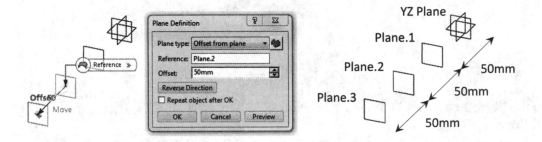

Pick the yz plane from the tree, or the screen, and select

the "Positioned Sketch" icon 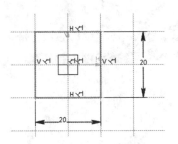 from the bottom row
menu (i.e., action bar). Note that the "Positioned Sketch"
is in the "Model" tab. This will land you in the Sketcher
App.
Draw a 20 mmx20 mm square, centered at the origin.

Exit the sketcher ⬆ Exit Add.

Select the Plane.1, and enter the sketcher Positioned Sketch... . Draw a 20
mmx20 mm square, centered at the origin just like above.
We would like to rotate this sketch by 10 degrees
counterclockwise.

Select the "Rotate" icon 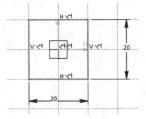 from the action bar menu.

You are prompted to select the entities to be rotated. Choose the four sides of the square as shown.

There is also an obscure instruction in the bottom left corner of the screen (the prompt area), asking to select the center of rotation Select or click the rotation center point . With the cursor, select the origin of the sketch plane. This was the reason behind centering the square.

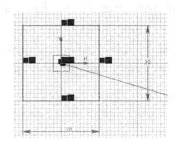

Make sure that the "Duplicate mode" box is unchecked and for the "Value" input 10 degrees.

Uncheck, otherwise the original square also remains

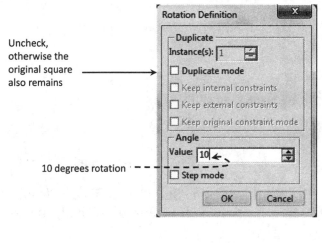

The result of the rotation is shown below.

10 degrees rotation

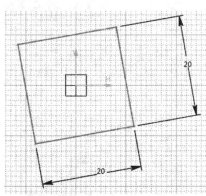

Exit the Sketcher 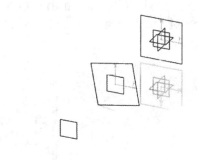.

Repeat the process for Plane.2 and Plane.3, creating the same size rectangles and rotate by 20 and 30 degrees.

Original 20X20mm rectangle

Original 20X20mm rectangle, rotated 10 deg

Original 20X20mm rectangle, rotated 20 deg

Original 20X20mm rectangle, rotated 30 deg

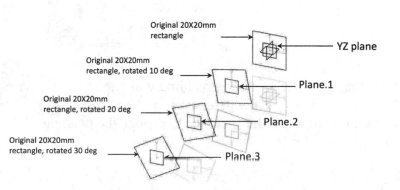

YZ plane

Plane.1

Plane.2

Plane.3

The tree structure at this point is shown below.

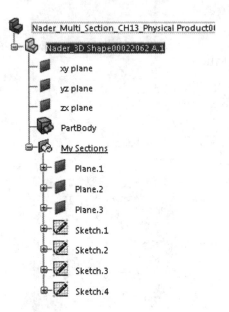

Select the "Multi-sections Solid" icon 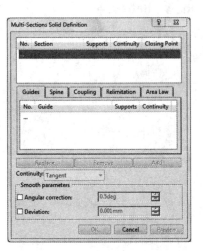 leading
to the "Multi-Sections Solid Definitions" dialogue box.

Select the four sketches from the screen and press "OK."
The shape of the part generated is shown below.

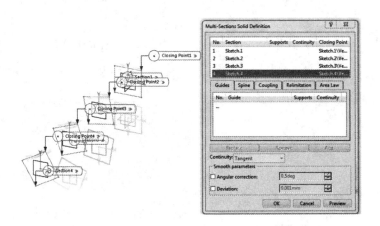

Note that the solid section is residing with the
PartBody and not the geometric set. In the next page
you will manipulate the sketches to change the twisting
shape of the object.

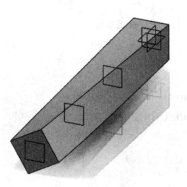

Double click on the object (or the corresponding branch of the tree) to open the dialogue box.

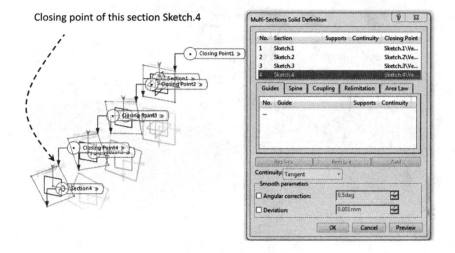

Closing point of this section Sketch.4

First make sure that Sketch.4 is showing. If necessary, place the cursor on the Sketch.4 branch, right click, "Show."

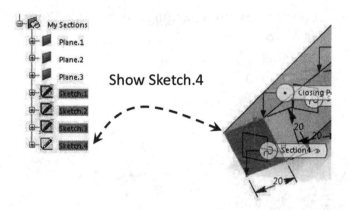

Show Sketch.4

Place the cursor on the current "Closing Point," right click and select "Replace." You will then have the opportunity to select a different "Closing Point."

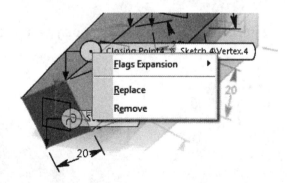

Use the cursor to select the new "Closing Point." See the next page.

Select this vertex as the new "Closing Point"

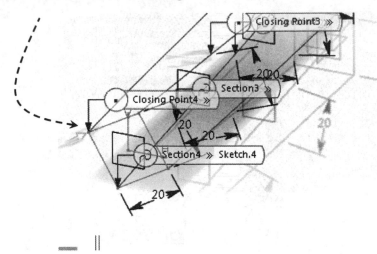

Repeat this process for changing the "Closing Point" of the Sketch.1 which has the YZ Plane as its "Support."

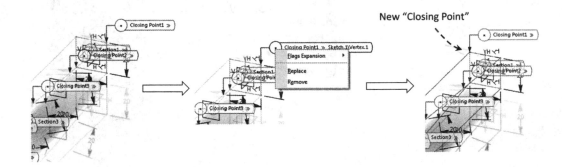

The resulting highly twisted geometry is shown below.

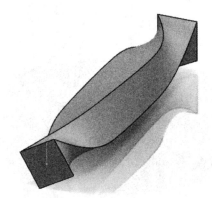

In the remaining part of this chapter, there will be an attempt to briefly outline the idea behind "Removed Multi Sections Solid." The strategy is to create a rectangular base first.

First deactivate the multi section solid just created. Select the branch, right click, "Deactivate."

The multi section solid disappears from the screen.

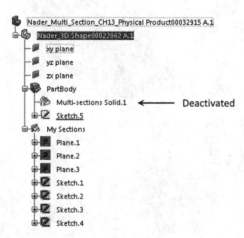

Deactivated

Select the YZ plane and enter the sketcher. In the sketcher, draw a rectangle as shown and dimension it.

Exit the sketcher and "Pad" 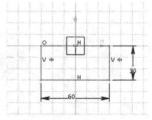 the rectangle by 150mm.

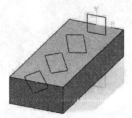

Select the "Removed Multi-Solids Section" icon 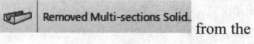 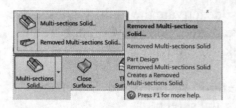 from the menu.

In the resulting dialogue box, select the four sketches from the tree or the screen and press "OK."

The modified base is shown below.

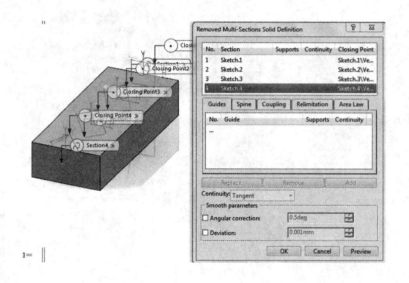

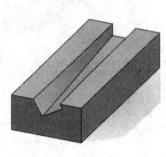

Exercise 1:

The objective of this exercise is to create a twisted blade using the "Multi-Sections Solid" functionality. The final product is shown below and you can use dimensions of your own choice.

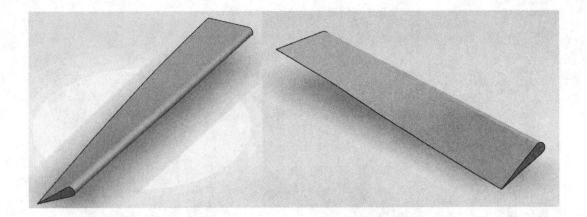

Hint: In the next few lines, we propose a strategy to achieve the goal of the exercise.

1- Construct five equally spaced parallel planes.
2- On one of them draw a sketch of the cross sectional profile.

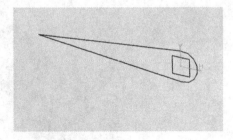

3- Project the profile drawn on the next plane.
4- Use the "Isolate" icon to detach the sketch from its source.
5- Select the profile (all edges) and rotate them by a given angle.
6- Repeat steps 3 through 5 for the next plane.

7- Use the "Multi-Sections Solid" icon to create a solid out of the five profiles.
8- You may have to adjust the "closing Points" to avoid a highly twisted solid.

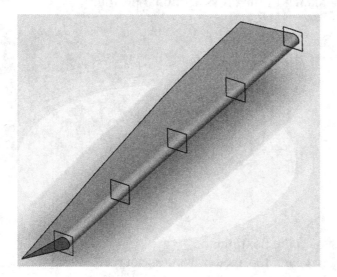

Surfaces,
Generative Shape Design App

Objective:

Up until this point, we have been primarily dealing with solid geometries. However, there is a large class of structural components that are more efficiently modeled as thin sheets. To name a few, one can mention sheet metals, instrument panels, ship hulls, and aircraft fuselage. To accommodate such structures, surfaces are used for idealizing the geometry. In 3DEXPERIENCE, basic surfacing is handled by the Generative Shape Design Application. The objective of the present chapter is to have a quick tour of this application. Dimensions are not important in this chapter as only the functionalities will be shown.

The Generative Shape Design App:

From the extensive list of applications in the V+R section of the compass, select

"Generative Shape Design" icon _{Shape Design} to enter the App. Along with some utility tabs, the action bar at the bottom of the screen has three major tabs, namely, the Wireframe, Surface, and Volume. These are shown below.

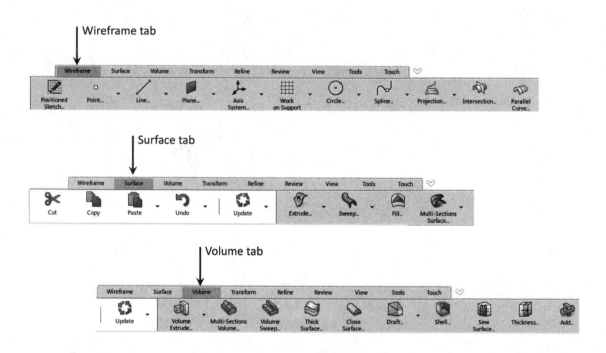

Some of the Volume capabilities are also available in the Part Design App, but in principle, the concepts of "Volume" and "PartBody" are completely different. The more sophisticated surfacing and volume functionalities can be found in "Aesthetical Shape Modeler" and "Class A Modeler Apps." The present basic book is not the proper forum to discuss these specialized tools.

Creating a Surface with "Fill" :

Choose the Wireframe tab from the action bar. Selecting the "Point" icon , create four points with the coordinates (0,0,0), (0,1,0), (1,1,0), (1,0,0.5). Note that the last point does not lie in the plane generated by the first three.

Create four lines connecting these points consecutively as shown.

Select the "Fill" icon 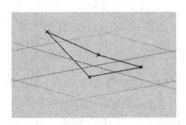 from the action bar menu (Surface tab).

In the resulting dialogue box, select the four lines just generated. A surface is placed on the four lines.

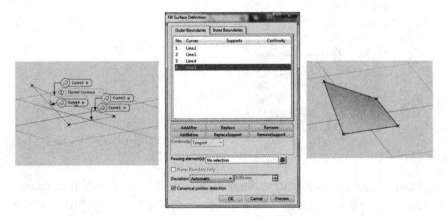

Keep in mind that "Fill" can be used for any closed curve in space. Here is a more complicated filled surface.

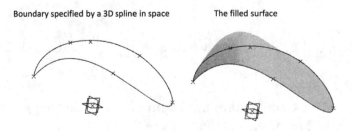

Boundary specified by a 3D spline in space

The filled surface

Creating a Surface with "Extrude" :

Choose the Wireframe tab. Select the
YZ plane and enter the sketcher and draw a
spline curve as shown and exit the sketcher.

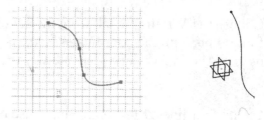

Select the "Extrude" icon from the action bar menu (Surface tab). For the "Profile"
select the spline just sketched and for the "Direction" place the cursor in the blank space,
right click, and select the X Component. Depending on where you generated the spline,
your direction may have to be specified differently.

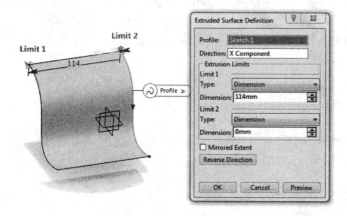

The "Extrude" operation in the Generative Shape Design App is the counterpart
of "Pad" in the Part Design App. The direction of extrusion is along a straight line. If the
extrusion is to be along a curved path, the "Sweep" operation can be used.

Creating a Surface with "Sweep" :

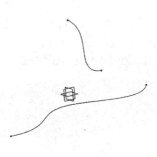

Draw another arbitrary spline path as shown on
the right. The original spline was in the yz plane and the
new spline (the path along which sweeping will take
place is in the xy plane).

Select the "Sweep" icon  from the action bar (Surface tab). This leads to a rich dialogue box shown on the right. We will perform a very basic sweep and therefore will not worry about the different options.

For the "Profile" select the original spline drawn in the yz plane, and for the "Guide curve" select the second spline drawn in the xy plane.

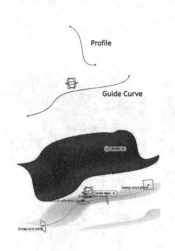

The final surface due to the above sweep is shown below. Note that on the top left margin of the dialogue box there are several options that one can be using. The surface below

used the default which is the left most choice .

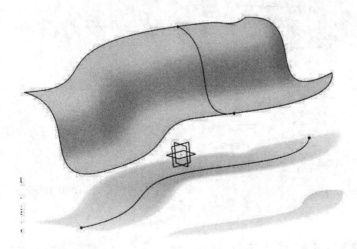

Creating a Surface with "Revolve" :

You will be using the same spline that was drawn in the yz plane. Select the "Revolve" icon  from the Surface tab of the action bar.

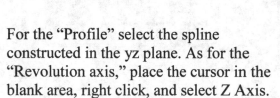

For the "Profile" select the spline constructed in the yz plane. As for the "Revolution axis," place the cursor in the blank area, right click, and select Z Axis.

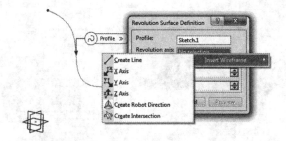

The revolved surface is shown below.

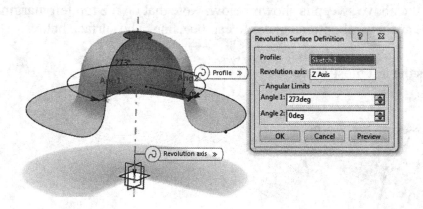

Creating a Surface with "Multi-Sections Surface" :

Consider the four sections (three rectangles and a circle) shown on the right. The intention is to make a surface passing through these sections.

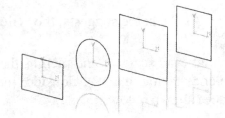

Select the "Multi-Sections Surface" icon  from the action bar menu.

In the resulting dialogue box, select the four sections as shown. Keep in mind that the "Closing point" location can have a dramatic impact on the generated surface. This point can be changed as discussed in the Multi-Sections Solids in an earlier chapter. The shape of the generated surface and several different views are shown below.

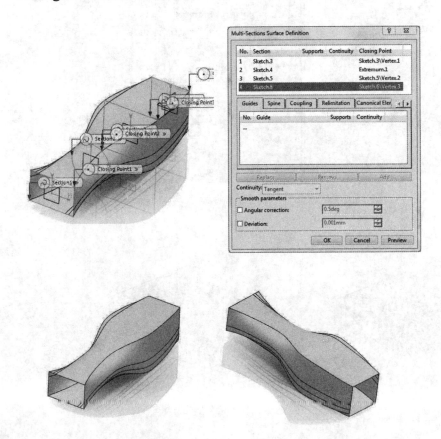

Blending Surfaces with "Blend" :

As the name suggests, the "Blend" icon

 takes to surfaces and merges them together
(or blends them together). Consider the two
surfaces shown below.

Select the "Blend" icon and in the resulting dialogue box make the selections shown. The
blended surfaces and their different renderings are shown below.

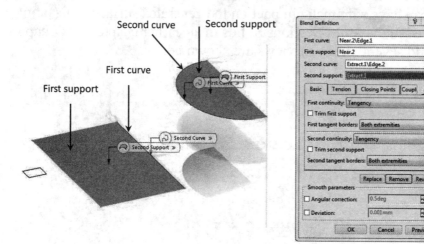

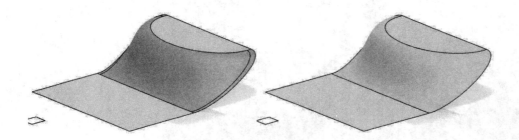

Creating a Surface with "Extract" :

> In some situations, one has a three dimensional solid part and may be interested to extract some surfaces associated with the solid. This is achieved through the "Extract" icon .

To explain the process, first make a sketch similar to what is shown below and pad it to create a solid object.

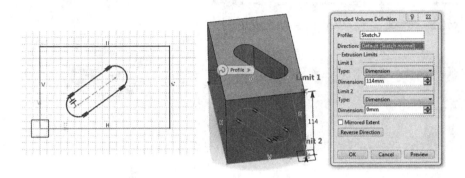

In the Generative Shape Design App, select the "Transform" tab.

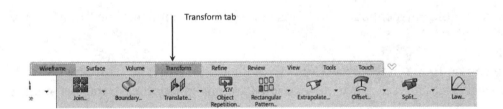

Select the "Extract" icon from the action bar menu. For the "Element(s) to Extract" select the top face of the block. The extracted surface is shown below.

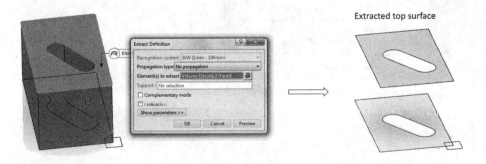

Extracted top surface

If there are several surfaces to be extracted, this process has to be repeated as many times as needed. A more efficient way is to use the

"Multiple Extract" icon from the same menu. The figure below shows three surfaces extracted simultaneously.

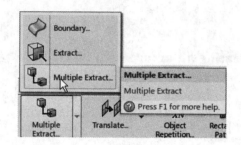

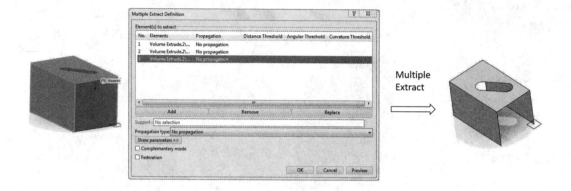

Joining Surface **Join...** :

One can assemble adjacent surfaces to make up one element using the "Join" icon

 Join... .

The "Join" icon can be found in the Transform tab of the action bar. The figure below shows how the surfaces that were just multi-extracted are joined together to make a single surface.

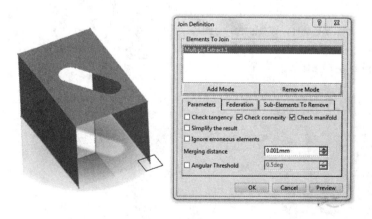

"Offset" a Surface to Create Another Surface :

Consider the single surface that was obtained by the "Join" operation just completed. Select the "Offset" icon in the Transform tab. For the "Surface" select the joined surface created earlier and as the "Offset" input 30 mm. A new surface is created as shown below.

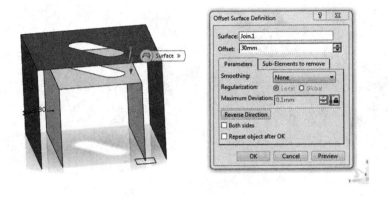

"Extrapolate" a Surface to Create a New One :

Given a surface, under normal circumstances one can extend the surface with the "Extrapolate" icon which is in the "Transform" tab. The figure below shows that the top surface (with the selected boundary) has been extrapolated by 132 mm.

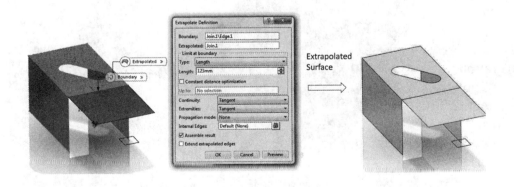

Splitting a Surface with another Element **:**

The "Split" icon which resides in the "Transform" tab allows you to split (or cut) a surface with another surface. Consider the situation below. The extrapolated surface (Extrapolate.1) already created is to be split with the surface of the revolution (Revolute.1) which was created earlier in the chapter.

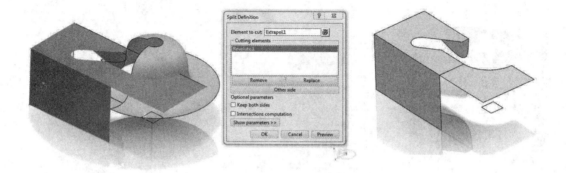

Select the "Split" icon. For the "Element to cut" use "Extrapolate.1" and for the "Cutting elements" select "Revolute.1." The result of this operation is displayed on the right-hand side of the figure above.

"Symmetry" Functionality for Mirroring **Symmetry...** **:**

This is a very useful tool to mirror surfaces with respect to a plane.

For demonstration purposes, the Split.1 surface just created has been mirrored to generate a more complicated surface.

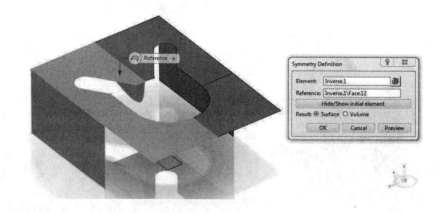

Scaling of Surfaces  :

In certain situations, a surface needs to be scaled up (or down) to meet its

functional requirements. This is where the "Scaling" icon Scaling... can be quite handy. For illustration purposes, consider the mirrored surface which was just created (see above). Use the "Scaling" icon with the selections shown below to scale down the left side of the combined surface.

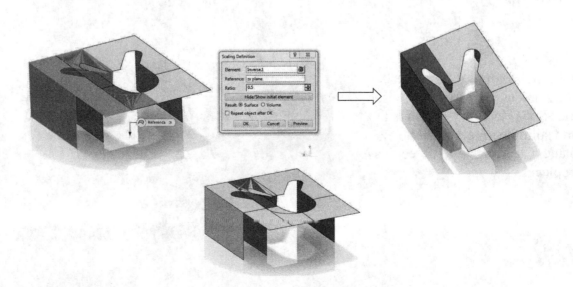

Creating Solid Object with "Close Surface" :

      This feature is used when a surface can be closed in order to make a solid object. Note that for this operation to be possible, a surface must meet certain requirements. For example, a flat rectangular surface cannot be closed regardless.

Consider the surface shown below; clearly it can be closed by capping the two ends.

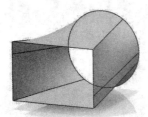

Select the "Close Surface" icon from the action bar. For the "Surface to close" choose the open surface above. The software creates the caps as surfaces, and therefore closes the surface, and even more importantly, creates a solid object out of the closed surface.

Solid Object

To convince the reader that a solid object exists, we have used the "Split" icon in the Solids tab and split the object with the yz plane. Clearly a solid object was in place.

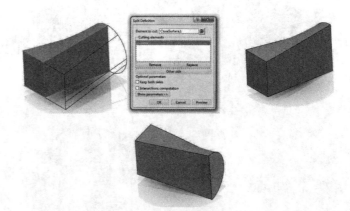

Sewing a Surface to a Volume   :

Let us suppose that a user wants to apply a pressure load on a circular region on the top face of the block shown below. In a majority of modern CAE software, if the surface on which the point "A" is located is selected, the pressure is applied on the entire surface. To a typical user, a way to get around is to create a feature around the point "A" such as the circular stand displayed in the figure, and then apply the pressure on the created circular surface. This strategy is referred to as an "embossment" in the CAD terminology. Although this may be reasonable in certain problems, it could be problematic in general. For example, stress concentration may be resulting due to the height of the padded/extruded embossment.

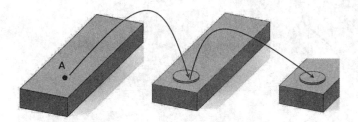

There are specific approaches to avoid this issue which are software dependent and the users should be made aware of them. In the 3DEXPERIENCE program, the process involves creating a circular surface on the top face which obviously has no height, and "sewing" the created surface to the top face of the block. This creates a feature to which the pressure load can be applied. The steps for this process are outlined below in detail. In the "Volume" tab of the action bar, create a block. On the top face of the block, draw a

circular sketch. Using the "Fill" icon   in the "Surface" tab, create a circular surface on the circle drawn.

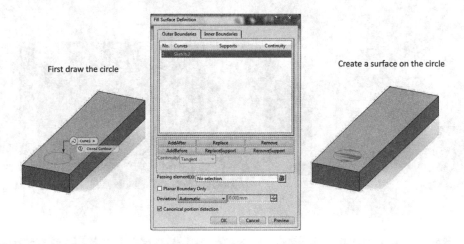

Select the "Solid" tab of the action bar. Now use the "Sew Surface" icon 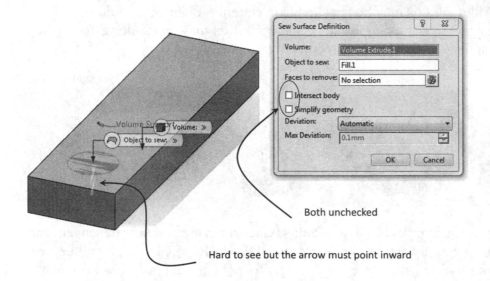 to open the dialogue box below. For the "Volume," pick the block which was created in this App (not in the Part Design). For the "Object to Sew," choose the "Fill" surface which was put on the circle.

Make sure that the two boxes are both unchecked. Finally, there is an arrow originating at the sewed surface (the "Fill" here). This arrow, which is difficult to see on the screen, must point into the block. Press "OK" and you are done.

To make sure that everything worked satisfactorily, the block has been meshed (the circular feature is recognized), and a pressure can be imposed solely on the circular patch.

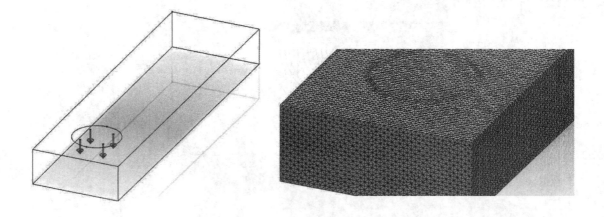

Exercise 1

In this exercise you will be experimenting with the "Multi-Sections Surface" functionality further. Specifically, the role of the "Spine" curve will be explored. The first step is to create three parallel planes 50 mm apart. This can easily be one by creating offsets of the YZ plane. There is no particular significance to the dimensions that are referred to in this exercise.

Within each one of these planes draw three semi-circles with radii, 20 mm, 15 mm and 5 mm as shown.

In the XY plane, you can draw an arbitrary curve (say a spline) with an approximate configuration shown.

This spline will be used as the "Spine" of the surface, or its "Guide curve."

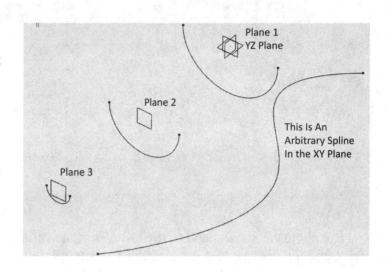

Using the "Multi-Sections Surface" icon 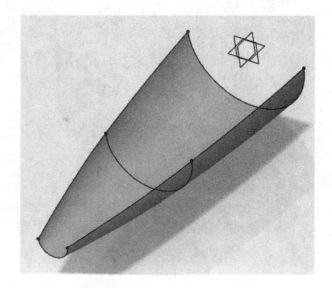, pick the three arcs and let 3DEXPERIENCE create the lofted surface as shown below. Ignore the spline curve for now.

As a second attempt, select the "Spine" tab in the bottom portion of the dialogue box and pick the spline in the XY Plane.

You can see the dramatic change in the shape of the lofted surface displayed on the next page.

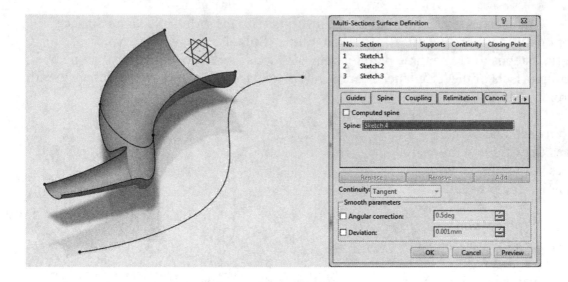

The sectional curves which lead to the lofted surface can be dramatically different. As an example, change the two end semi-circles to rectangles and observe the effect. In dealing with such surfaces, the "Closing Point" plays a major role and can lead to unacceptable twisted surfaces. The surface below was generated without specifying a "Spline."

One other point to mention is that the sketched surfaces do not have to lie in parallel planes and the "Spine" does not have to be a planar curve.

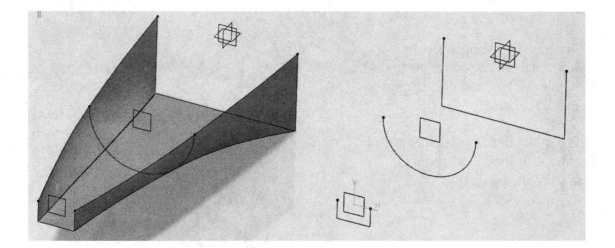

Slider Crank Assembly

Objective:

In this tutorial, you will manipulate four solid objects to assemble them as a slider crank mechanism. It is assumed that you have already created and saved the four 3D Shapes with the software. The Assembly Design App is the tool from 3DEXPERIENCE that is used to achieve the above goal.

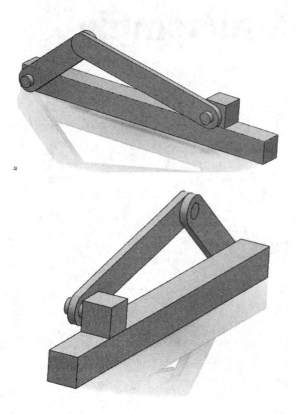

Geometrical Dimension:

Although the dimensions of the components are irrelevant to the process (but not to the kinematics), the tutorial details provide some specific dimensions making it easier for the reader to model the appropriate parts.

Where specific dimensions are given, it is recommended that you use the indicated values (in inches). Some dimensions of lesser importance are not given; simply estimate those dimensions from the drawing.

The 3D Shapes (parts) are named Nader_Base, Nader_Crank, Nader_Conrod, and Nader_Piston as shown below.

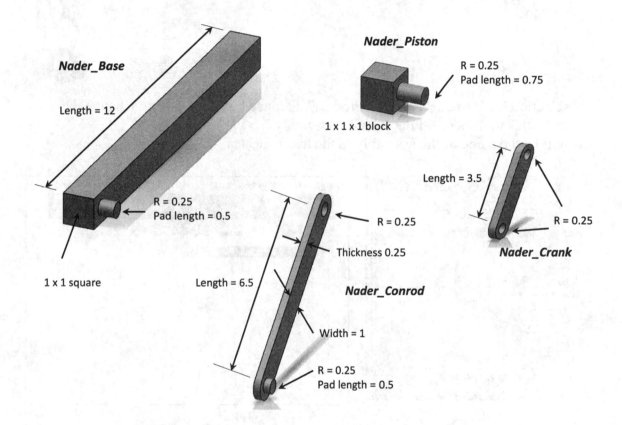

Creation of the Assembly 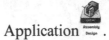 **:**

Click on the WEST sector of the compass on the
top left corner of the screen. This will open the
CAD applications available in 3DEXPERIENCE.

From the list, select the "Assembly Design"

Application 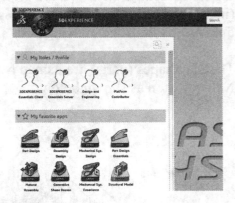.

This selection leads to the "Physical Product" dialogue box shown next. Change the
default "Title" to "Nader_Slider_Crank_Assembly."
This will be the name of the assembly as the tree indicates.

The parts are already generated and stored in the "cloud" database. They need to be
retrieved and inserted in the assembly.

Place the cursor on the assembly name "Nader_Slider_Crank_Assembly," right click,
select "Insert," followed by "Existing 3D Part" as shown on the next page.

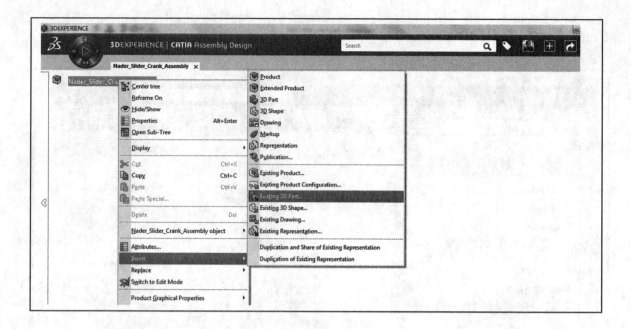

The window on the screen asks you to search for the parts to be inserted. In order to look for the parts, place the cursor in the "Search" area, left click, and select "My Content."

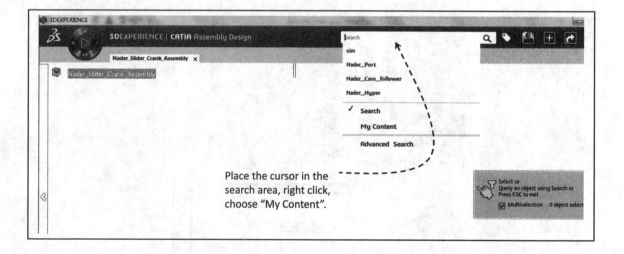

Place the cursor in the search area, right click, choose "My Content".

Since there are four parts to be retrieved, it is more efficient to use the "Multiselection" option. Recall that "Multiselection" of entities in 3DEXPERIENCE is achieved by holding the Ctrl key down while picking the entities of interest.

A view of your search area appears on the screen. This consists of all files in your "My Content" of the "cloud" database.

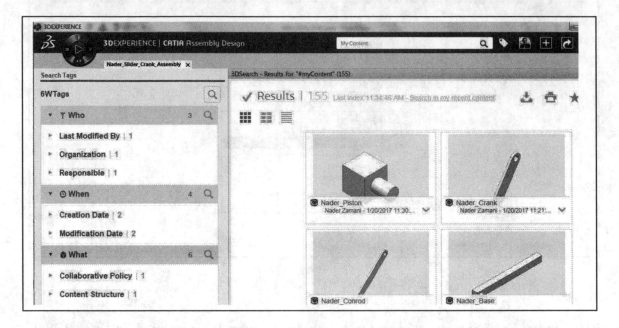

The files of interest are to be located. These part files are Nader_Piston, Nader_Crank, Nader_Conrod, and Nader_Base. Select them one by one with the Ctrl key down during the selection.

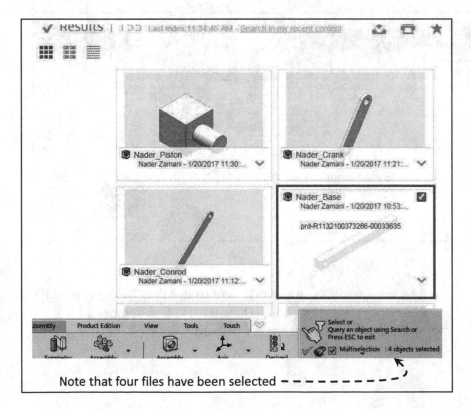

Note that four files have been selected – – – – – – – – –

Before pressing the "Enter" key on the keyboard, you have the opportunity to review your selections from the expanded window on the right. If satisfactory, click on the green check mark.

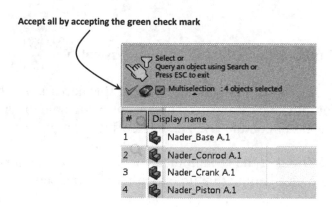

You will then see all the inserted parts appear on the screen and recorded in the tree.

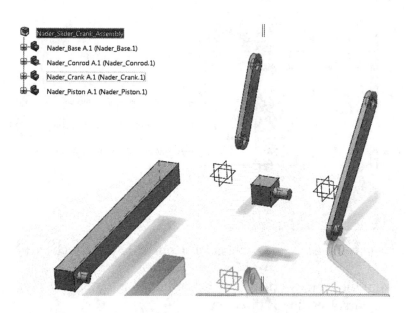

To avoid a busy screen, you can always "Hide" some of the parts. In the view below, the piston and connecting rod have been hidden.

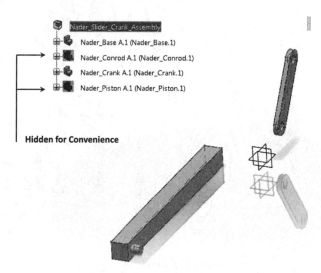

Manipulating Parts Within an Assembly :

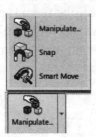

In dealing with assemblies, it is necessary to be able to manipulate parts easily. This means being able to translate and rotate them on the fly. The most effective tool for performing such operations is the "Manipulate" icon. In the next paragraph the basic idea behind this functionality is explained.

Once the "Manipulate" icon is selected, the following pop-up box appears. This box has thirteen functionalities to choose from. These are described below.

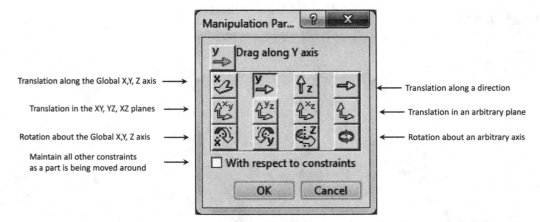

As an example, suppose we want to translate the part Nader_Conrod in the direction +Z.

You select the button from the window, place the cursor on the part, and select it by a left click. Finally, drag the cursor in the +Z direction.

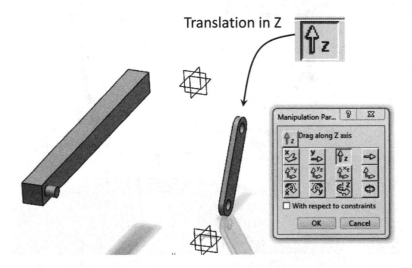

Applying Assemble Constraints (Engineering Connections) :

Fixing Nader_Base:

The features "Engineering Connection" and "Fix" in many other software are referred to "Assembly Constraints." In the present problem, the part Nader_Base is to be fixed or anchored. This means that the particular part is remaining fixed in its original location as other engineering connections are being imposed.

The first task is to fix this part. Select the "Fix" icon 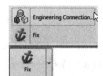 from the menu and then pick the part Nader_Base from the screen or the tree.

The tree confirms that Nader_Base has been fixed. Note that the imposed constraint (Fix) appears within the part Nader_Base and in the bottom of the tree where all assembly constraints are recorded.

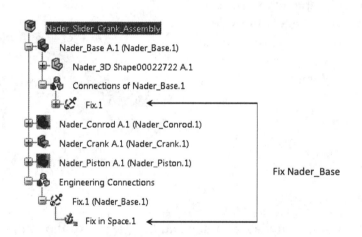

Fix Nader_Base

Revolute Joint between Nader_Base and Nader_Crank:

Select the "Engineering Connection" icon 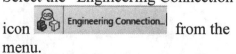 from the menu.
This leads to the "Engineering Connection Definition" dialogue box. Note that the "Type" currently says "User Defined."

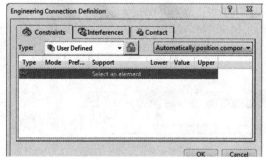

If you know what kind of joint is to be created, you can select it from the pulldown menu. Otherwise, leave it as "User Defined" and proceed. The software will automatically detect the appropriate joint.

First select the axis of the embossment in the Base and then the axis of the hole in the crank (or, the inside surface of the hole of the crank). Immediately you will see that the two axial locations line up.

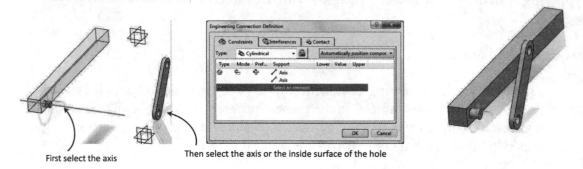

First select the axis   Then select the axis or the inside surface of the hole

First note that the "Type" of the joint automatically changed to "Cylindrical." Another point to make is that the automatic update of assembly constraints can be deactivated by the user if desired. This can be done through the "Preferences" menu.

The next step is to select two faces. First select the side face of Nader_Base and then the back face of Nader_Crank.

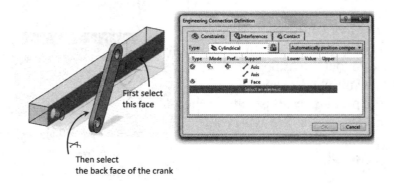

First select this face

Then select the back face of the crank

An automatic update is made and the "Type" of the joint changes to "Revolute."

In this step, you will be faced with the pop-up window below. Close the window by pressing the "Yes" button.

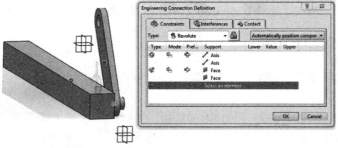

Checking the tree reveals the revolute joint between Nader_Base and Nader_Crank has been created.

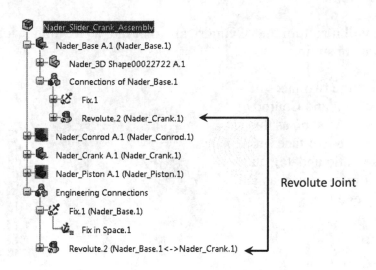

Revolute Joint

Revolute Joint between Nader_Crank and Nader_Conrod:

Since the next joint involves the part Nader_Conrod, we have to bring it out of the "Hide" mode.

Select the "Engineering Connection" icon

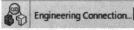 from the menu.

Choose the axis of Nader_Crank followed by the axis of the embossment in Nader_Conrod.

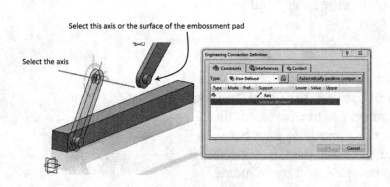

The update is automatically done, the two parts line up as expected, and the "Type" changes from "User Defined" to "Cylindrical."

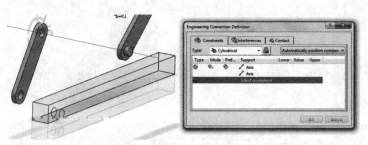

We will next turn the "Cylindrical" joint into a "Revolute" joint by invoking plane to plane constraints.

Select the two faces of the Crank and Conrod as shown. As soon as this is done, the two faces mate (automatic update), and the joint type is changed to "Revolute."

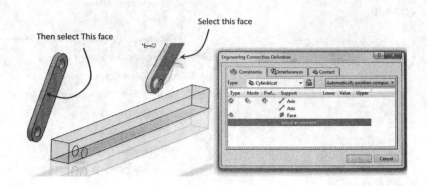

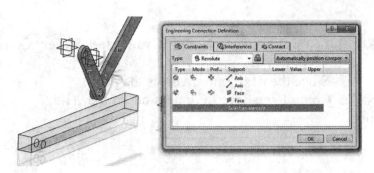

In this step, you will be faced with the pop-up window on the right. Close the window by pressing the "Yes" button.

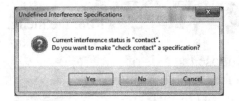

Note that although the revolute joint between the Crank and the Conrod has been created, the previous revolute joint between the Base and the Crank needs updating. Select the "Update" icon [] to achieve this.

After the Update Operation

It is a good idea to use the "Manipulate" icon [Manipulate...] to roughly position the parts in their natural configuration. This can save the user a great deal of headaches downstream.

1. Select the "Manipulate"

   icon 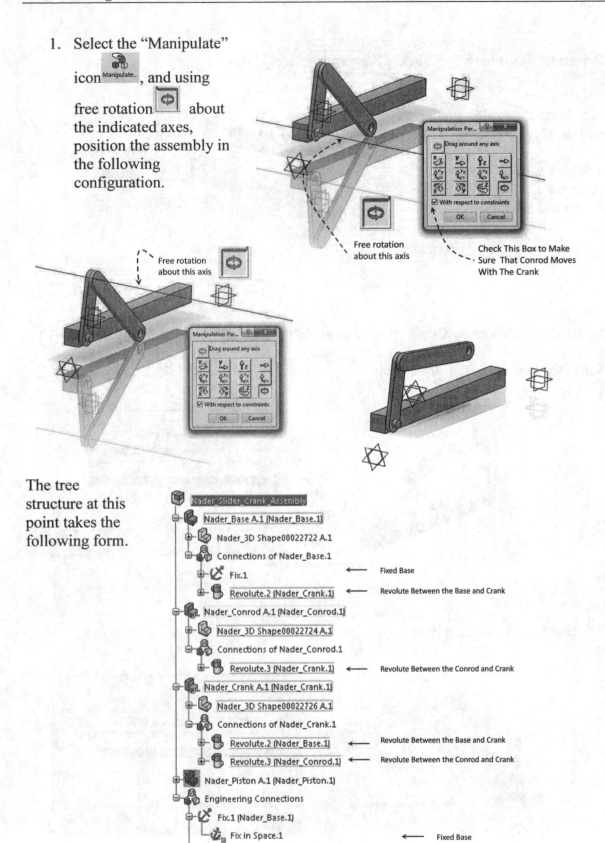, and using

   free rotation about
   the indicated axes,
   position the assembly in
   the following
   configuration.

Free rotation
about this axis

Free rotation
about this axis

Check This Box to Make
Sure That Conrod Moves
With The Crank

The tree
structure at this
point takes the
following form.

Nader_Slider_Crank_Assembly

   Nader_Base A.1 (Nader_Base.1)

      Nader_3D Shape00022722 A.1

      Connections of Nader_Base.1

        Fix.1 ← Fixed Base

        Revolute.2 (Nader_Crank.1) ← Revolute Between the Base and Crank

   Nader_Conrod A.1 (Nader_Conrod.1)

      Nader_3D Shape00022724 A.1

      Connections of Nader_Conrod.1

        Revolute.3 (Nader_Crank.1) ← Revolute Between the Conrod and Crank

   Nader_Crank A.1 (Nader_Crank.1)

      Nader_3D Shape00022726 A.1

      Connections of Nader_Crank.1

        Revolute.2 (Nader_Base.1) ← Revolute Between the Base and Crank

        Revolute.3 (Nader_Conrod.1) ← Revolute Between the Conrod and Crank

   Nader_Piston A.1 (Nader_Piston.1)

   Engineering Connections

      Fix.1 (Nader_Base.1)

        Fix in Space.1 ← Fixed Base

      Revolute.2 (Nader_Base.1<->Nader_Crank.1) ← Revolute Between the Base and Crank

      Revolute.3 (Nader_Crank.1<->Nader_Conrod.1) ← Revolute Between the Conrod and Crank

Prismatic Joint between Nader_Base and Nader_Piston:

First bring the Nader_Piston
into the show mode.

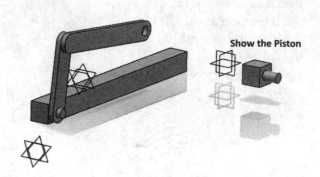

The plan is to create a
"Prismatic" joint between the
Piston and the Base.

Select the "Engineering Connection" icon 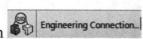 from the menu.

Select the bottom face of the Piston.

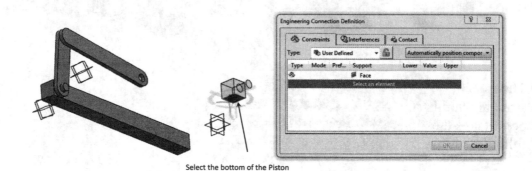

Select the bottom of the Piston

Select the top face of the Base.

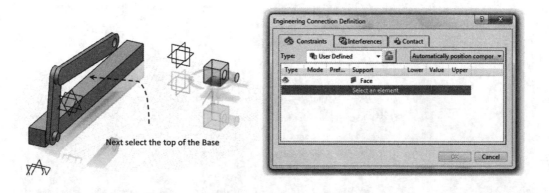

Next select the top of the Base

As soon as the two faces are selected, the joint type changes to "Planar."

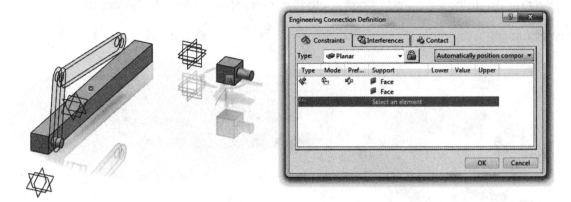

Next, we need to select the appropriate edges of Nader_Piston and Nader_Base.

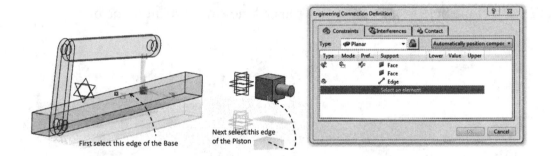

The assembly immediately gets updated to account for the newly created "Prismatic" joint.

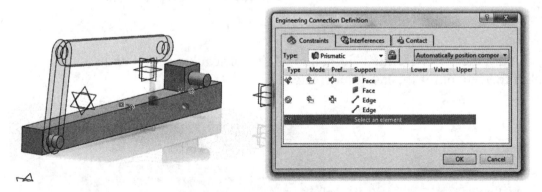

Close the "Undefined interference Specifications" dialogue box by pressing "Yes."

Cylindrical Joint between Nader_Conrod and Nader_Piston:

This is the final joint needed to complete the assembly constraints. Select the "Engineering Connection" icon [Engineering Connection...] from the menu.

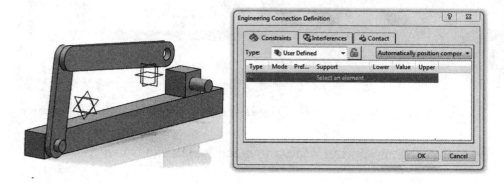

Select the axis of the hole in the connecting rod and the embossment in the piston.

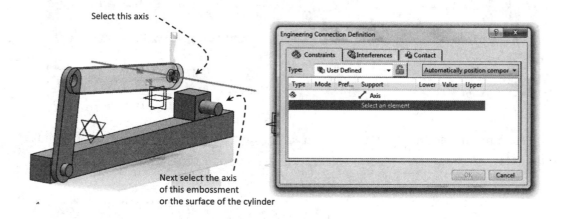

This will turn the "User Defined" joint into a "Cylindrical" joint and updates the assembly to account for the last joint created.

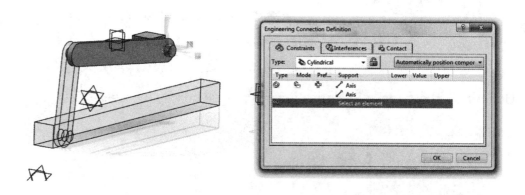

Close the "Undefined interference Specifications" dialogue box by pressing "Yes."

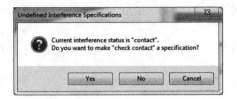

Note that although the cylindrical joint just created has been correctly updated, the prismatic joint now has to be manually updated. Select the "Update" icon ⟳ to achieve this.

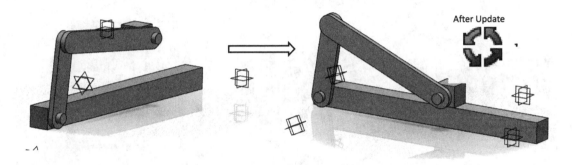

The complete tree structure is now shown below.

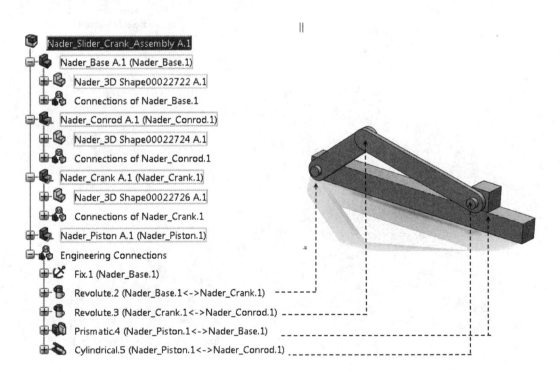

Checking Your Assembly Constraints Collectively:

One way to check your assembly, to ensure that all the constraints are holding, is the use

of the "Manipulate" icon 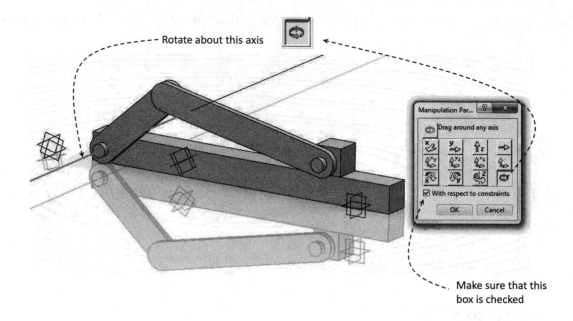. Select the "Manipulate" icon.

Use the free rotation about the selected axis, and rotate the Crank. The whole structure
must move in unison confirming the validity of the constraints.

Rotate about this axis

Make sure that this
box is checked

Exercise 1: Analog Clock Mechanism

Using dimensions of your choice, model and create the following assembly.

Exercise 2: Rack Pinion Assembly

Using dimensions of your choice, model and create the following assembly.

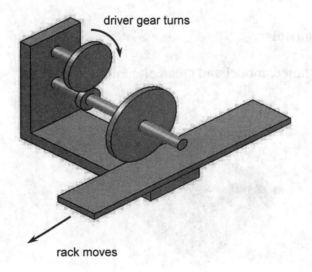

Exercise 3: Sliding Ladder, with Wheels

Using dimensions of your choice, model and create the following assembly.

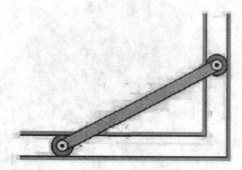

Exercise 4: The Sliding Bar

Using dimensions of your choice, model and create the following assembly.

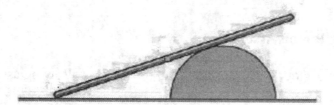

Exercise 5: Geneva Mechanism

Using dimensions of your choice, model and create the following assembly.

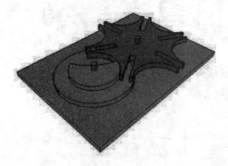

Robotic Arm Assembly

Objective:

In this chapter, a model is developed of a three degree of freedom robot consisting of two revolute joints and a prismatic joint. This robot configuration is often referred to as a SCARA (Selective Compliance Assembly Robot Arm) type of robot. This is representative of a number of typical robotic assembly tasks such as dispensing adhesives, hemming sheet metal, etc.

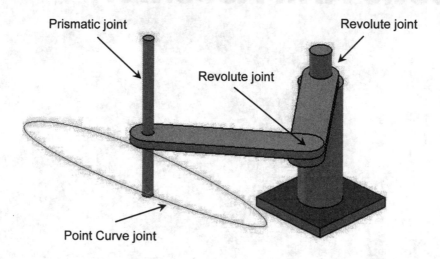

Prismatic joint

Revolute joint

Revolute joint

Point Curve joint

Geometrical Dimension:

The geometrical dimensions associated with the five parts making up the assembly are shown below. Some dimensions of lesser importance are not given; simply estimate those dimensions from the drawing. Although both the dimensions and the units are irrelevant for pedagogical reasons, the units are assumed to be in meters.

The reader is expected to be able to create these five parts and store them on the "cloud." The parts are then read into an assembly where constraints are imposed.

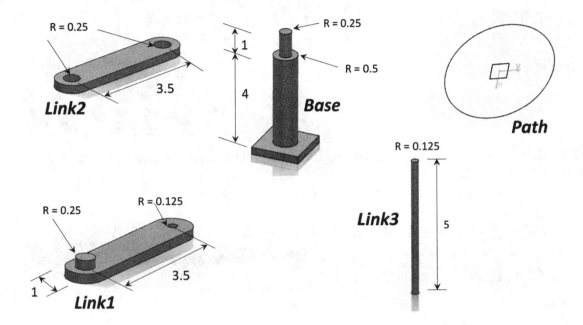

Creation of the Assembly 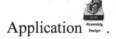 :

Click on the WEST sector of the compass on the
top left corner of the screen. This will open the
CAD applications available in 3DEXPERIENCE.

From the list, select the "Assembly Design"

Application 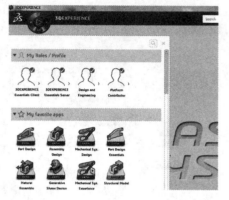 .

This selection leads to the "Physical Product" dialogue box shown next. Change the
default "Title" to "Robotic_Arm."
This will be the name of the assembly as the tree indicates.

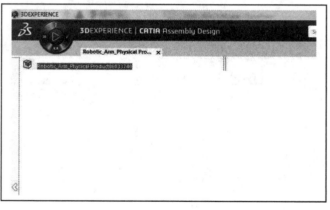

The parts are already generated and stored in the "cloud" database. They need to be
retrieved and inserted in the assembly.

Place the cursor on the assembly name "Robotic_Arm," right click, and select "Insert"
followed by "Existing 3D Part" as shown on the next page.

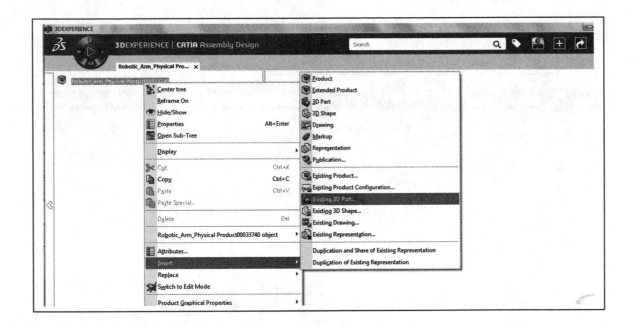

The window on the screen asks you to search for the parts to be inserted. In order to look for the parts, place the cursor in the "Search" area, left click, and select "My Content."

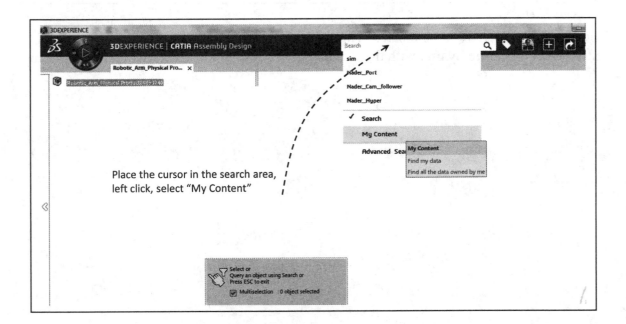

Since there are five parts to be retrieved, it is more efficient to use the "Multiselection" option. Recall that "Multiselection" of entities in 3DEXPERIENCE is achieved by holding the Ctrl key down while picking the entities of interest.

A view of your search area appears on the screen. This constitutes of all files in your "My Content" of the "cloud" database.

The files of interest are to be located. These part files are Base, Link1, Link2, Link3, and Path. Select them one by one with the Ctrl key down during the selection.

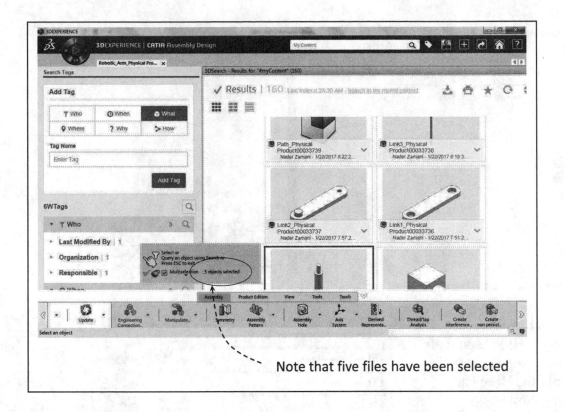

Note that five files have been selected

Before pressing the "Enter" key on the keyboard, you have the opportunity to review your selections from the expanded window on the right. If satisfactory, click on the green check mark.

Accept all by clicking on the green check mark

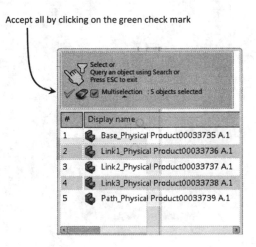

You will then see all the inserted parts appearing on the screen and recorded in the tree.

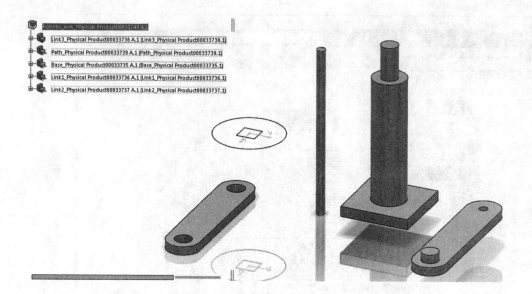

To avoid a busy screen, you can always "Hide" some of the parts. In the view on the right, only the Base and Link1 are showing.

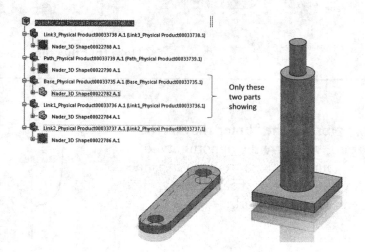

Only these two parts showing

Applying Assembly Constraints (Engineering Connections) :

Fixing the Base:

The features "Engineering Connection" and "Fix" in many other software are referred to "Assembly Constraints." In the present problem, the part Base is to be fixed or anchored. This means that this particular part is remaining fixed in its original location as other engineering connections are being imposed.

The first task is to fix this part. Select the "Fix" icon  from the menu and then pick the part "Base" from the screen or the tree.

The tree confirms that Base has been fixed. Note that the imposed constraint (Fix) appears within the part Base and in the bottom of the tree where all assembly constraints are recorded.

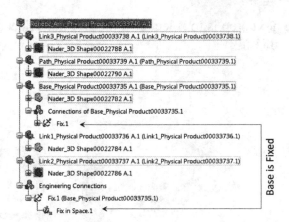

Revolute Joint between Base and Link1:

Select the "Engineering Connection" icon 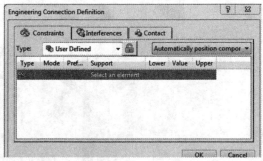 from the menu. This leads to the "Engineering Connection Definition" dialogue box. Note that the "Type" currently says "User Defined."

If you know what kind of joint is to be created, you can select it from the pulldown menu. Otherwise, leave it as "User Defined" and proceed. The sotware will automatically detect the appropriate joint.

First select the axis of the Base and then the axis of the hole in the crank (or, the inside surface of the hole of Link1). Immediately you will see that the two axial locations line up.

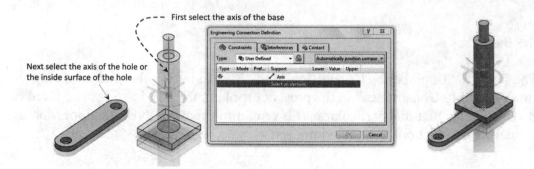

Note that the "Type" of the joint automatically changed to "Cylindrical." Another point to make is that the automatic update of assembly constraints can be deactivated by the user if desired. This can be done through the "Preferences" menu.

The next step is to select two faces. First select the circular top face of Base and then the face of Link1.

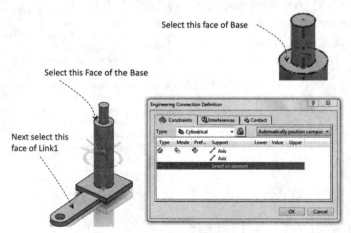

An automatic update is made and the "Type" of the joint changes to "Revolute."

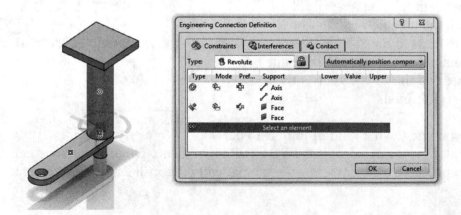

In this step, you will be faced with the pop-up window below. Close the window by pressing the "Yes" button.

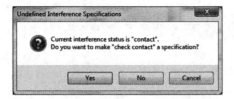

Checking the tree reveals the revolute joint between Base and Link1 has been created.

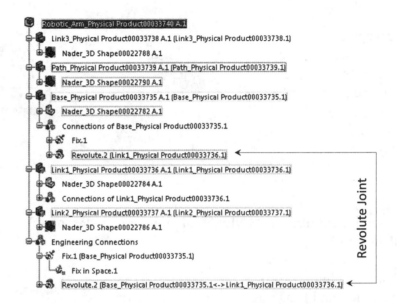

The updated configuration has been rotated to appear in its natural position as expected.

Revolute Joint between Link1 and Link2:

Since the next joint involves the part Link2, we have to bring it out of the "Hide" mode.

Select the "Engineering Connection" icon

 from the menu.

Choose the axis of the hole in Link1 followed by the axis of the embossment in Link2 (or the circular face of the embossment).

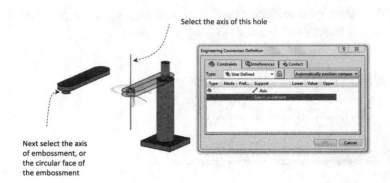

Select the axis of this hole

Next select the axis of embossment, or the circular face of the embossment

The update is automatically done, the two parts line up as expected, and the "Type" changes from "User Defined" to "Cylindrical."

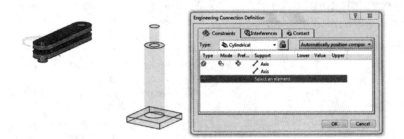

We will next turn the "Cylindrical" joint into a "Revolute" joint by invoking plane to plane constraints.

Select the two faces of the Link1 and Link2 as shown. As soon as this is done, the two faces mate (automatic update), and the joint type is changed to "Revolute."

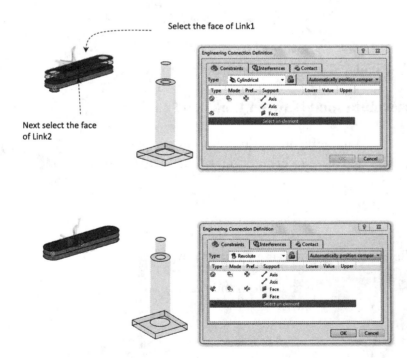

Select the face of Link1

Next select the face of Link2

In this step, you will be faced with the pop-up window below. Close the window by pressing the "Yes" button.

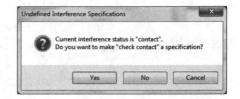

Note that although the revolute joint between the Link1 and the Link2 has been created, the previous revolute joint between the Base and the Link1 needs updating. Select the "Update"

icon ⟳ to achieve this.

After Update and Manipulation

It is a good idea to use the

"Manipulate" icon Manipulate... to roughly position the parts in their natural configuration. This can save the user a great deal of headaches downstream.

Select the "Manipulate" icon

Manipulate..., and using free rotation

⟲ about the indicated axis, position the assembly in the following configuration.

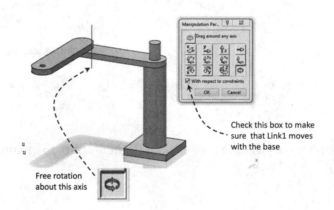

Check this box to make sure that Link1 moves with the base

Free rotation about this axis

Prismatic Joint between Link3 and Link2:

First bring the Link3 into the show mode.

The plan is to create a "Prismatic" joint between Link3 and Link2.

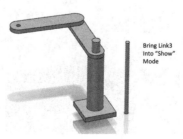

Bring Link3 Into "Show" Mode

Select the "Engineering Connection" icon 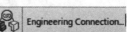 from the menu.

Select the axis of the hole in Link2 and the axis of Link3.

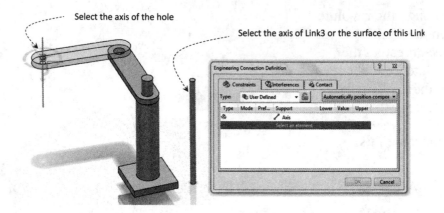

A "Cylindrical" joint between Link2 and Link3 is created.

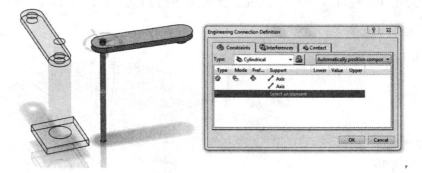

As soon as the two axes are selected, the joint type changes to "Cylindrical."

Next, we need to select the appropriate planes of Link2 and Link3 and make an angle constraint between them. Place the cursor on the line shown, right click, and follow the instructions to create the angle constraint.

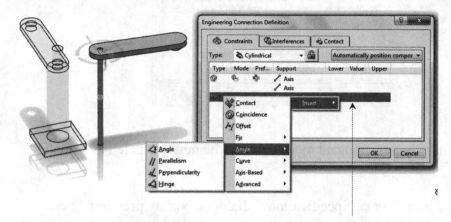

Place the cursor in this row, right click,
follow the trail to create an angle constraint

The planes to be taken to create the angle constraint are yz planes of Link2 and Link3. There are other possibilities depending on how the parts are oriented. This angle constraint forces the "Cylindrical" joint to become "Prismatic."

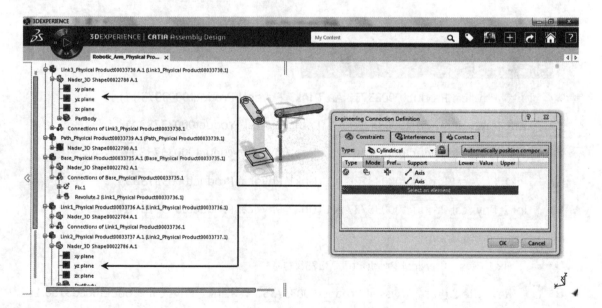

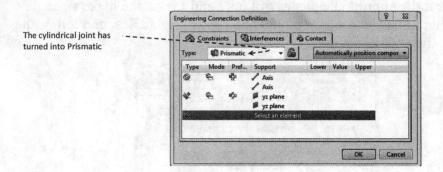

The cylindrical joint has turned into Prismatic

The assembly immediately gets updated to account for the newly created "Prismatic" joint.

Close the "Undefined interference Specifications" dialogue box by pressing "Yes."

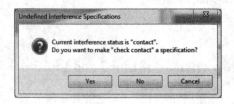

Select the "Update" icon 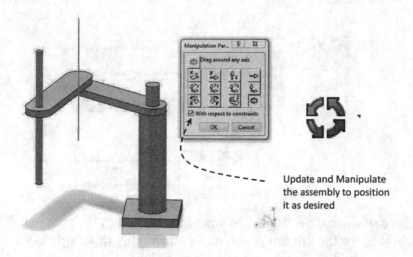 . Use the "Manipulate" icon to roughly position the parts in their natural configuration.

Update and Manipulate
the assembly to position
it as desired

Positioning the Path:

Bring the Path into the show mode.

The Path will be moved closer to the Base but the plane will also be rotated so that the resulting three dimensional path will be on a slanted orientation. The "Manipulate" icon will be used for positioning purposes.

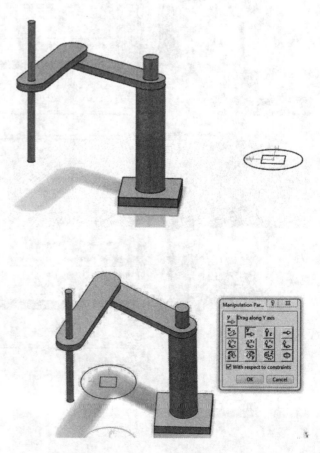

Select the "Engineering Connection" icon 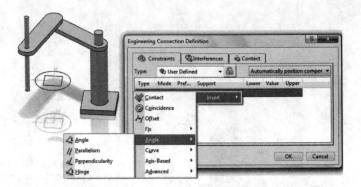 from the menu. When the dialogue box opens, position the cursor in the line shown, right click, and follow the trail to make an angle constraint. Select "Angle." You are expected to pick two planes and specify the angle between them.

Select the front vertical face of the base followed by the plane on which the path was drawn. There are other choices for the present problem. In our model, this angle is 90 degrees. The value is to be changed so that the plane becomes slanted.

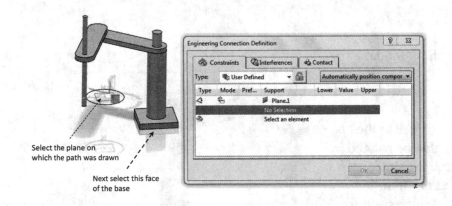

Select the plane on which the path was drawn

Next select this face of the base

Currently the angle between the two planes is 90 degrees. Change this angle to 45 degrees

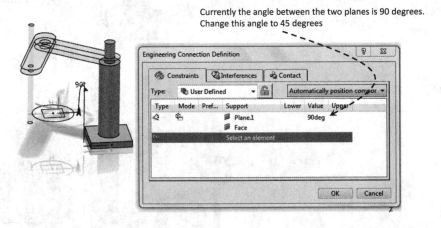

Place the cursor on the line where the current angle is specified; right click in the resulting window to change the angle to 45 degrees.

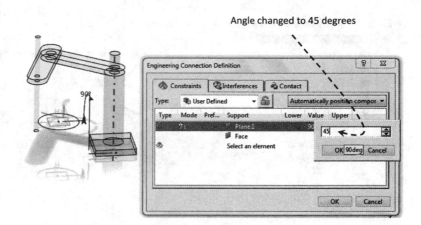

After closing this window (the change of angle window), you will see that the plane rotates and adjusts its angle to make 45 degrees with the front vertical face of the Base.

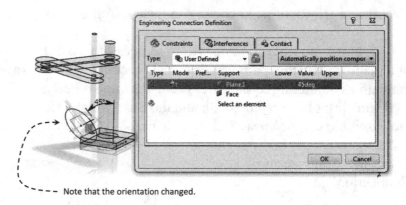

Note that the orientation changed.

Upon closing the "Engineering Connection Definition" and "Undefined Interference Specifications" windows, the assembly gets updated and ends up in the shown configuration. Note that the plane has rotated. The only remaining constraint is the point curve joint where the bottom of Link3 (the vertical link) touches the path. In order to impose this constraint, the reader must have already created a point at the bottom of the link (or it needs to be created at this point). Keep in mind that this point must belong to the Link3 part.

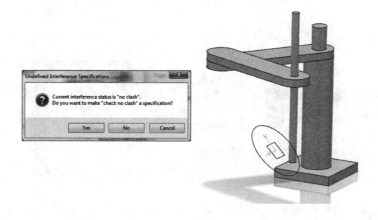

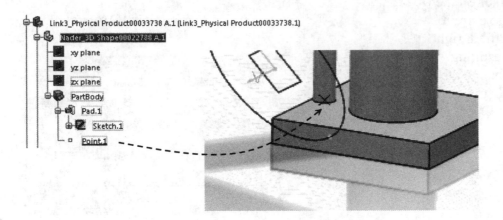

Creating a Rigid Joint between the Base and the Path:

In the present problem, we chose to create a part known as Path which consisted of a plane on which a path was drawn. This could have been avoided if we chose to draw the Path as belonging to the part "Base." However, because of our strategy, we can create a "Rigid" joint between the Path and the Base which effectively ties them together and the ensemble can be viewed as a single part.

Select the "Engineering Connection" icon 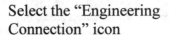 from the menu.
 From the pulldown menu select "Rigid."

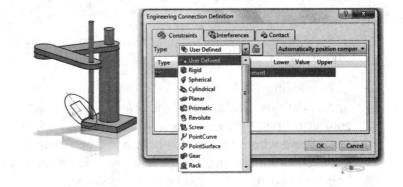

Select the Base from the tree

To create this joint, two entities have to be selected. From the tree, select Base, and for the second entity, select Path.

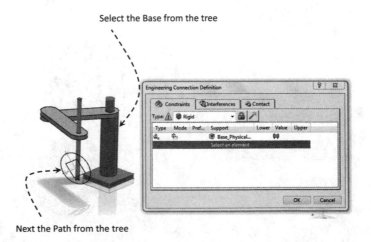

Next the Path from the tree

In the pop-up window which ensues, choose "New Connection."

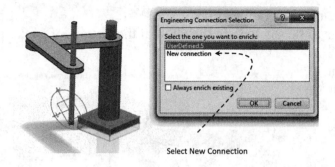

Select New Connection

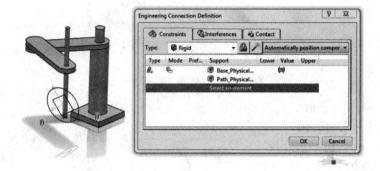

Upon closing the window, the two parts Path and Base become rigidly attached.

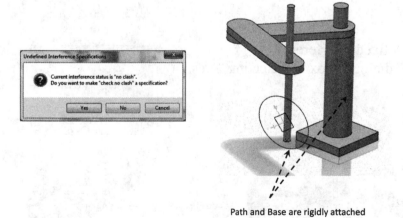

Path and Base are rigidly attached

Creating the Point-Curve Joint:

Select the "Engineering Connection" icon  from the menu. The two entities to be selcted are the point at the bottom of Link3 and the Path.

Select the Point.1 from the tree or the screen followed by the curve on the plane.

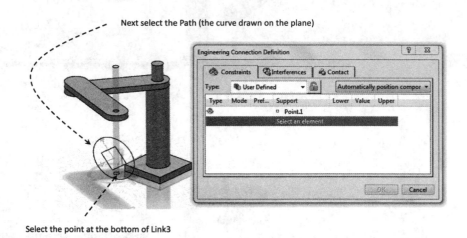

Next select the Path (the curve drawn on the plane)

Select the point at the bottom of Link3

You will see that the "User Defined" type joint immediately changes to a "PointCurve" joint.

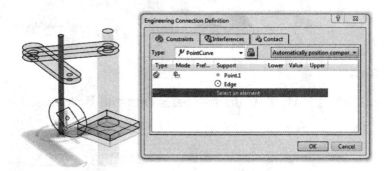

Close the "Undefined Interference Specifications" dialogue box by selecting "Yes."

Upon updating, the correct final configuration of the assembly is arrived at.

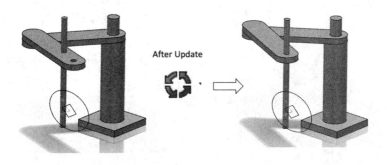

After Update

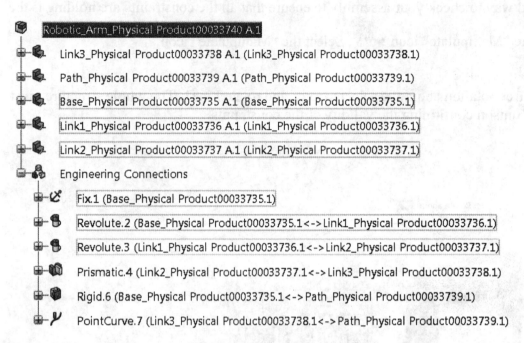

There are several ways to interrogate the software in order to find out whether all assembly constraints are holding or not. The First method is to use the "Manipulate" icon

, by moving the parts out of the intended position. After updating, all parts must snap back to the intended configuration.

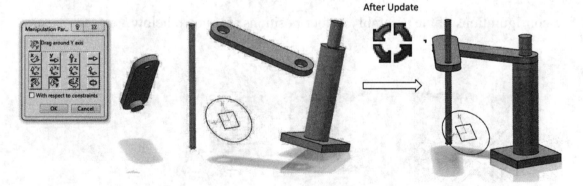

The second method which does not seem to be available in the Assembly Design App in 3DEXPERIENCE is the "Explode" view functionality. Using this feature, all the parts within the assembly are offset in the radial direction by a user specified value and center. This is commonly referred to as the "Explode" view. Upon updating, the parts should snap back to the original assembled configuration.

The third way to check your assembly to ensure that all the constraints are holding is the use of the "Manipulate" icon Manipulate... . Select the "Manipulate" icon.

Use the free rotation about the selected axis, and rotate Link1. The whole structure must move in unison confirming the validity of the constraints.

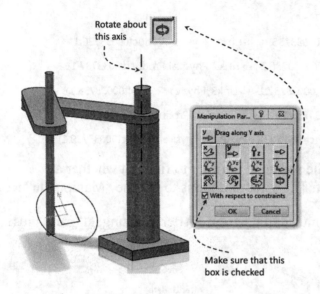

The configurations of the assembly at four positions are shown below.

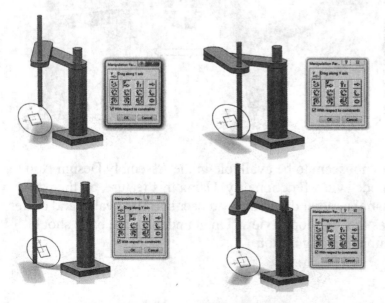

Exercise 1: The Shovel Mechanism

Using dimensions of your choice, create the following assembly.

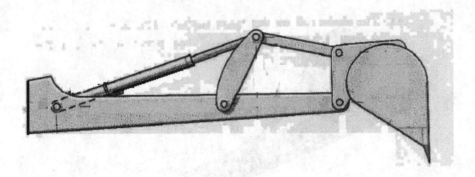

Exercise 2: The Rising Platform Mechanism

Using dimensions of your choice, create the following assembly.

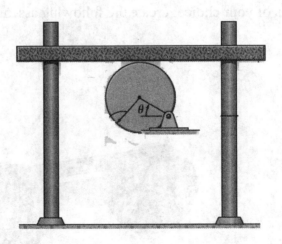

Exercise 3: Rolling Wheel Problem

Using dimensions of your choice, create the following assembly.

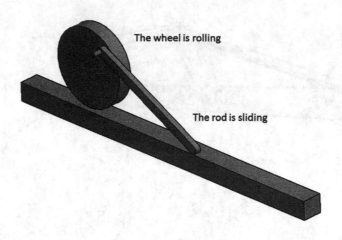

The wheel is rolling

The rod is sliding

Exercise 4: Locomotive Wheels

Using dimensions of your choice, create the following assembly.

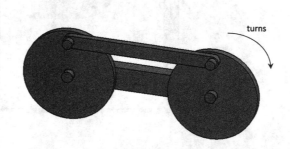

turns

Basic FEA for Designers

Objective:

At this point in the book, the reader is sufficiently familiar with the basic CAD functionalities in 3DEXPERIENCE to be exposed to a topic that is quite valuable in engineering design and product development. This topic is known as "Finite Element Analysis" or F.E.A. for short. In general, the FEA methodology is not considered as CAD and therefore not necessarily available in a CAD software. However, this functionality is available in 3DEXPERIENCE and quite easy to use.

The problem to be described in detail is the bar below, made of steel whose one end is clamped and the top face is exposed to a pressure of 1 MPa. The steel is assumed to behave elastically with the Young's modulus and Poisson's ratio being $E = 200 \, GPa$ and $\nu = 0.3$. The objective is to find the tip deflection and the stress distribution in the beam. This problem is simple enough, that the subject of strength of materials has an approximate closed form solution for both quantities of interest.

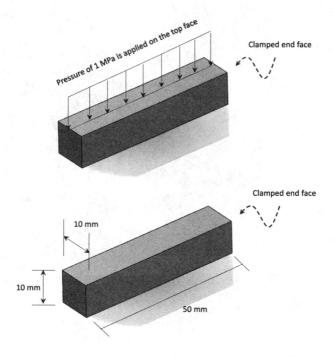

Some Comments about Doing FEA in 3DEXPERIENCE:

The subject of Finite Element Analysis is relatively new and its modern roots can be traced to the early 1960s. The rapid advancement of computing power has been the major factor in the FEA tool becoming widely used and available in the engineering/design circles. The rapid proliferation of FEA in the industrial daily life has also been responsible for serious abuse of the tool particularly in the interpretation of the results.

In order to use FEA effectively to solve engineering problems, it is wise to also learn the fundamental mathematics behind the tool, something that is often ignored by engineers and designers. In this chapter, we ignore the theory behind finite elements and demonstrate how to solve the cantilever problem in 3DEXPERIENCE.

The FEA engine within 3DEXPERIENCE is the Abaqus program by Simulia. However, there is also the stripped down version of Abaqus in a particular App in 3DEXPERIENCE. This particular application is known as the "Structural Validation"

Structural

App represented by the icon   Validation   . This particular App has severe limitations as an FEA software but is good enough for a rough analysis. These rough type analyses are precisely what is done by "Designers' these days. Needless to say, the other Apps shown below (also available in 3DEXPERIENCE) do not suffer from the above limitations.

Here are the other full blown FEA related applications in 3DEXPERIENCE.

Structural Model   Structural   Simulation   Physics Results
                        Scenario   Review

The focus of this chapter, however, is the "Structural Validation App." The readers who may also be interested in gaining more insight into FEA and Mechanism Design in 3DEXPERIENCE are encouraged to consult the following books by the current author.

Finite Element Essentials in 3DEXPERIENCE, by Nader G. Zamani, SDC Publications, 2017, ISBN 978-1-63057-100-9

Mechanism Design Essentials in 3DEXPERIENCE, by Nader G. Zamani, SDC Publications, 2017, ISBN 978-1-63057-104-7

Creating the Model and Applying Material Properties:

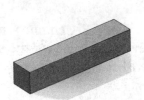

Using the Part Design App enter the sketcher, draw a 10 mm by 10 mm square, and pad it for 50 mm. The result is a box which will be your part.

The procedure for applying material properties is already discussed in an earlier chapter; however, due to its importance it is repeated here once again.

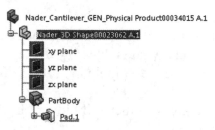

Select the "Tools" tab from the action bar.

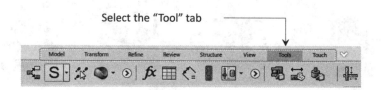

From the menu, choose the "Material Browser" icon . This opens up the expanded

section menu. Follow the steps shown below to select the "Create Material" .

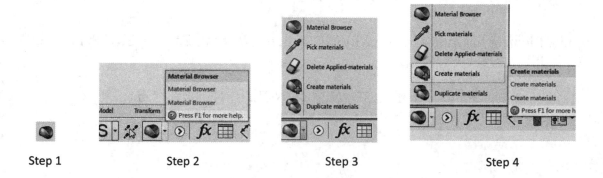

Step 1   Step 2   Step 3   Step 4

The selection of opens up a dialogue box shown on the next page. This box allows you to supply a proper name for the material should you decide to do so. Our assumption is that you do not have a material of interest in the "cloud" database and would like to follow the steps to create it. It is a rather tedious process but will be clearly spelled out.

Select the "Create Material" icon. Make sure that you check "Add domain" section and that the "Simulation Domain" is picked. Note that this creates a shell and the material information needs to be supplied later.

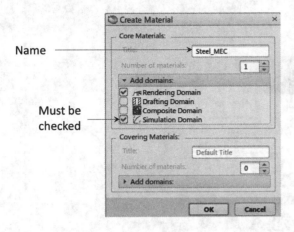

Once you close the dialogue box by clicking on "OK," you will find yourself in the material database and can identify the material that you just created, namely "Steel_MEC." The database screen is shown below.

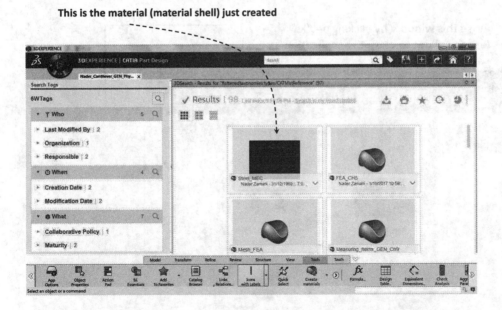

Place the cursor on your created material in the database, right click and select "Apply." You still have to return to the screen where the geometry exists and continue the work. This necessitates the closure of the current screen (the database screen).

Position the cursor here, on the screen, right click, select "Apply"

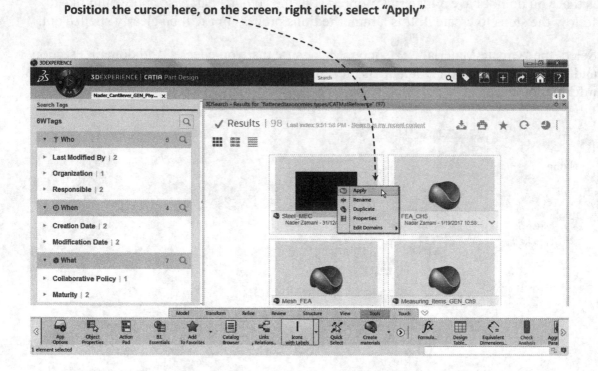

Select the "X "on the top right margin of the database screen to close the window. You will return to the geometry window; however, the shape of the cursor is modified as shown on the right.

Close this window by clicking on "X."
Be careful not to close the application instead.

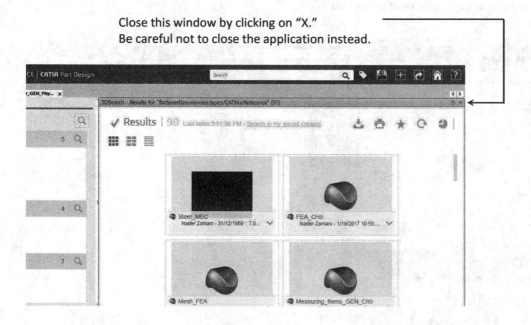

Place the cursor on the part (on the screen or on the top branch of the tree) and double click.

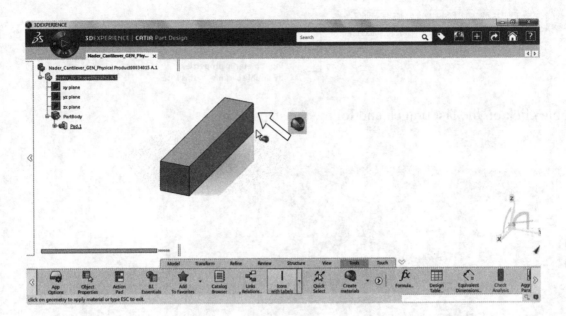

You will notice that the "Materials" branch is created at the very bottom of the tree as shown below. You can then use the cursor to select the "Green" check mark to proceed.

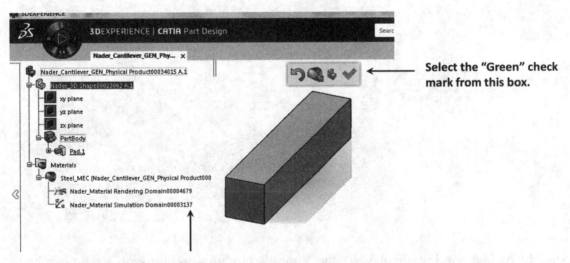

Please note that the actual material properties are yet to be inputted. Expanding the "Materials" branch reveals two other branches. The location where the properties are inputted is the last branch "Nader_Material Simulation Dommain00003137" as shown above.

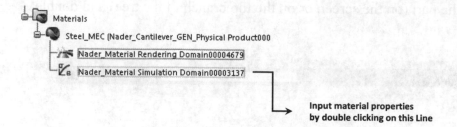

Input material properties
by double clicking on this Line

Double click on the last branch and follow the steps below.

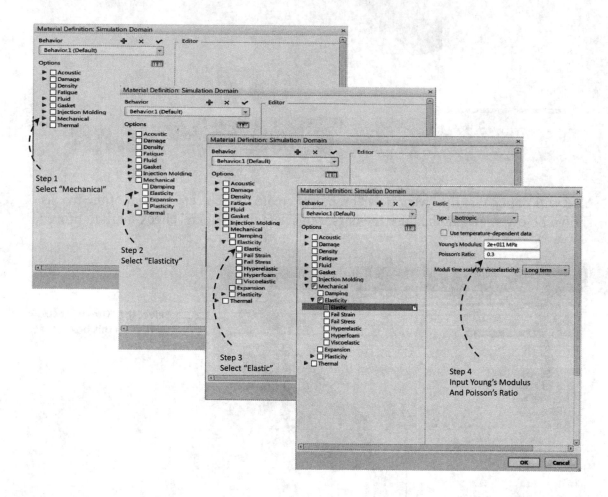

In Step 4 (the last window displayed), the Young's modulus and Poisson's ratio can be inputted. For the present problem, use $E = 2 * 10^{11} \ Pa$ and $\nu = 0.3$ which are the standard values for carbon steel. Properties can be changed by simply double clicking on the last branch show.

Entering the Structural Validation App:

Locate the compass on the top left corner of the screen, and select the South sector (i.e., V+R sector) as shown on the right. Scroll through the applications and select the Structural Validation

App   **Structural Validation**   .

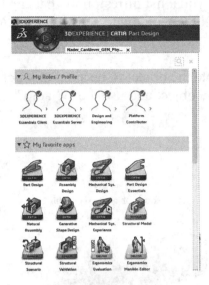

You are prompted to select the appropriate analysis. The present problem is a structural one and therefore the default is fine.

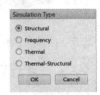

The "Wizard" appears in the top right margin of your screen which will guide you through the steps. Notice the material is already checked because it was created. The concept of "Connections" does not apply to the present problem.

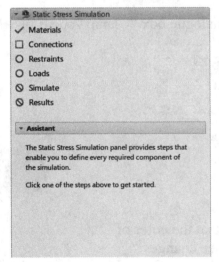

The action bar in the bottom of the screen has the following appearance.

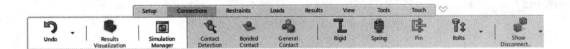

Select the "Restraints" line from the wizard and it will give you a list of restraints that can be used. You can scroll the window to see all the choices.

Rotate the object to be able to select the appropriate face of the object and use the "Clamp" box to apply.

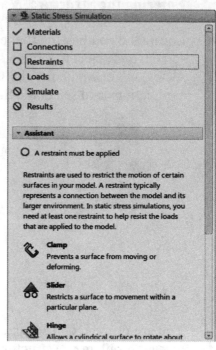

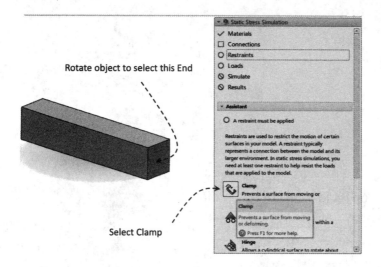

The dialogue box "Clamp" opens up where you can pick the appropriate face to be fixed.

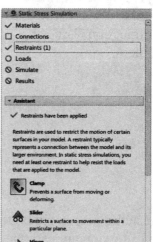

Note that the color of that face changes (slightly to indicate that it is clamped) and a green check mark in "Restraints" appears.

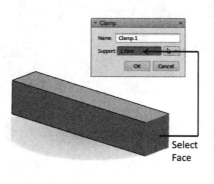

In the wizard, select the line dealing with "Loads." If you scroll down the list, you will find all types of loads that can be applied in this application.

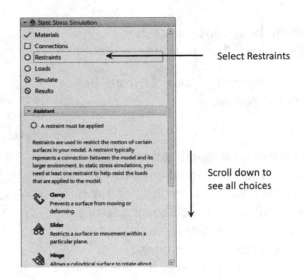

In the present problem, a pressure loading of 1 MPa is applied to the top face of the cantilever beam.

Select the "Pressure" icon from the list, and pick the top face of the cantilever beam with the cursor. Type in "1 MPa" for the magnitude of the pressure. Note that the color of the top face slightly changes (to indicate that load was applied to the face). Furthermore, a green check mark appears in front of "Loads" on the top section of the wizard window.

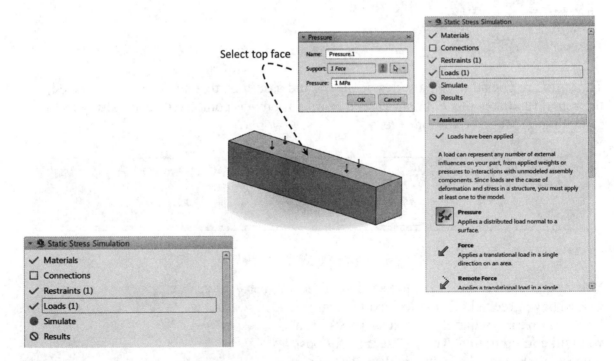

The wizard indicates that "Simulate" is the last step. Simulate means that the FEA software is to be run to produce the results.

From the wizard, select the
"Simulate" line from the top section,

followed by the icon 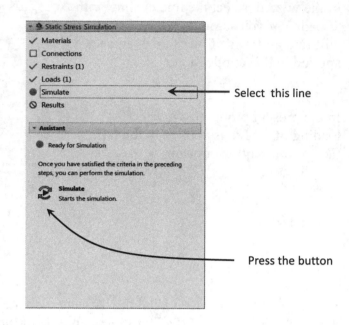 from the
bottom section.

In the pursuing dialogue box, you
need to indicate the degree of
accuracy that you are looking for.
Naturally, the more accurate results
require longer running time. Since
this chapter is for demonstration
purposes, you can specify "Draft."

The software goes through a series of checks and assuming that no errors are detected,
the actual run takes place. In our case, the simulation was completed successfully as the
following dialogue boxes indicate.

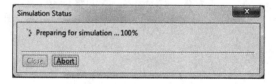   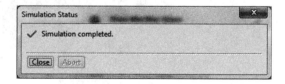

First note that all items in the top section of the
wizard have green check marks next to them.
Furthermore, immediately after a successful run,
you will end up in the "Results" section for post
processing. In fact, the software displays the von
Mises stress as the default stress.

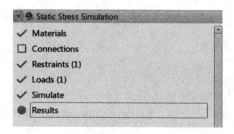

The plot of von Mises stress is shown below.

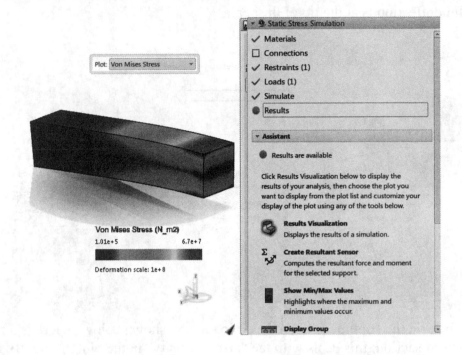

Using the "Plot" pull down menu, you can select other entities to be plotted. For example, "Displacement" is one that is commonly looked at. The displacement plot is shown on the next page.

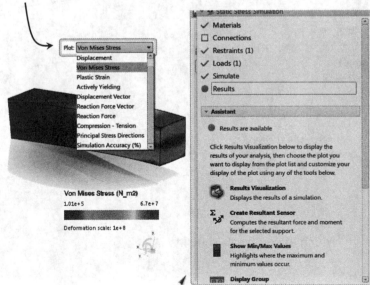

The "Displacement Vector" plot is not in the contour format but it is a vector plot. This plot together with the "Zoomed" in version are shown below. Note that as expected, the maximum deflection is at the tip of the beam.

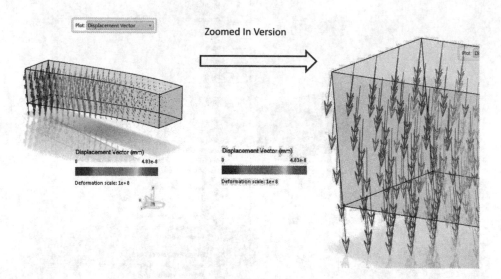

Double click on the contour to open the dialogue box shown below. There is a sliding bar in the bottom section; this deals with the "arrow density" in the plot. Currently it is at maximum. Drag it to the half way point and press "Apply." You will see that arrow density is reduced which may be of interest to the user.

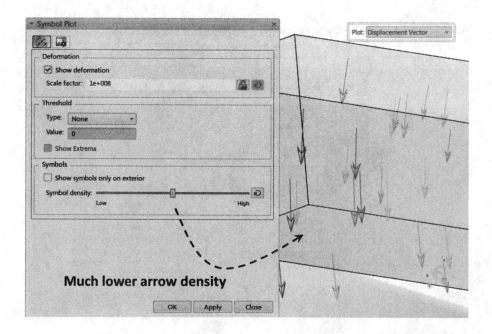

From the "Plot" pulldown menu, select
"Displacement" instead of "Displacement
Vector." The result is the contour plot of the
displacement field.

Very often it may be desirable to move the
contour legend (the contour guide with numbers
on it), or even make it bigger or smaller. In order
to do so, first select the legend by left clicking on
it. This will dim out the contour plot itself, as
shown below.

The dimming is the confirmation that the legend
has been selected.

Now hold the middle mouse button down,
which will allow you to pan (meaning moving
around).

If you select the contour legend, hold the middle
mouse button down, and a single click and
release of the right mouse button, you will be
able to make the legend bigger or smaller (zoom
in or out).

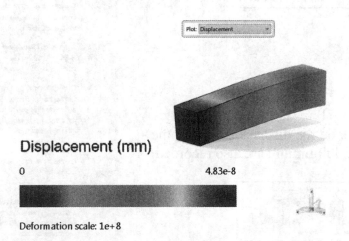

Displacement (mm)

0   4.83e-8

Deformation scale: 1e+8

When you are done with the manipulation of the contour legend, select it one more time
(for it to get released), and you are back to the contour plot itself.

Note that the contour plots that have been generated are shaded, i.e., the colors are not separated distinctly. Contour plots like this are referred to as "Smooth." It is possible to change this. Double click on the contour legend to open the dialogue box below.

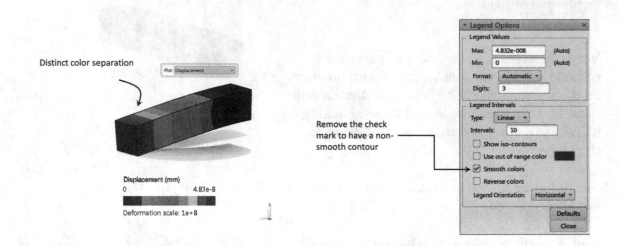

The complete list of items that can be used in the post processing is given below. Let us explore the "Show Min/Max Values."

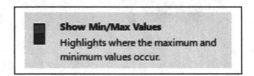

Click on this button.

You will see a pop-up box shown immediately below. Furthermore, on the displacement plot, the global maximum and minimum are also recorded.

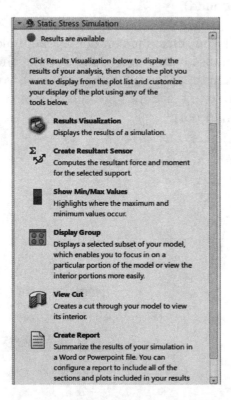

In the next page, the selection of each of these symbols is described through a series of plots.

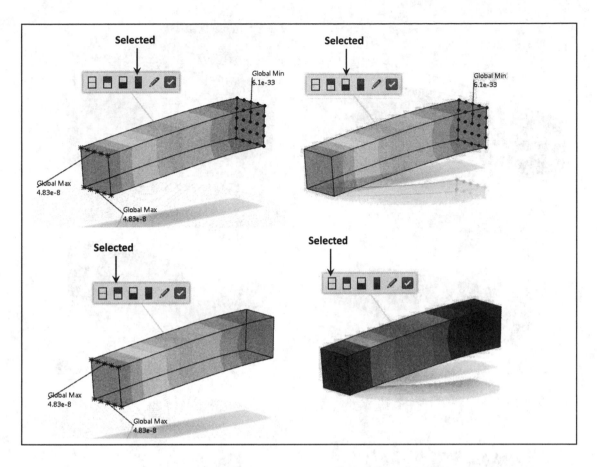

Once done with 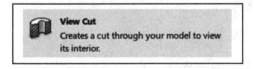 select the green check mark 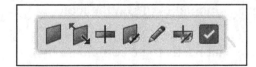 .

We will next explore the "View Cut" icon 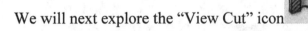 .

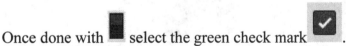

This feature allows you to make an arbitrary cut with a plane and explore the stress distribution inside of the part. The main menu for the "View Cut" icon is shown below.

In the next page, the selection of each of these symbols is described through a series of plots.

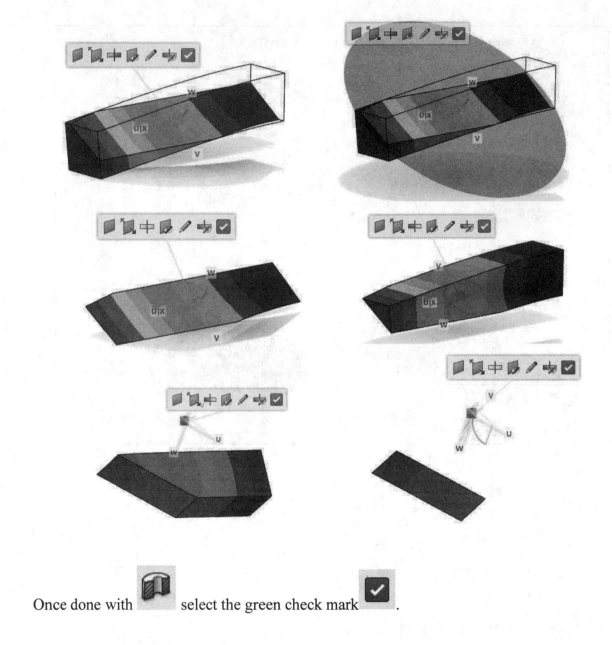

Once done with 📖 select the green check mark ✅.

The final item to be presented is the "Create Report" feature. This allows you to produce a professionally looking report from the FEA model generated and the selected results. The report can be custom made to meet your needs. This includes inserting company logo, personal information, and a menu to include/exclude the simulation results. The report can be generated in Word or Power Point formats. Upon clicking on the icon

"Create Report" 📄, the following dialogue box opens that needs to be completed by the user.

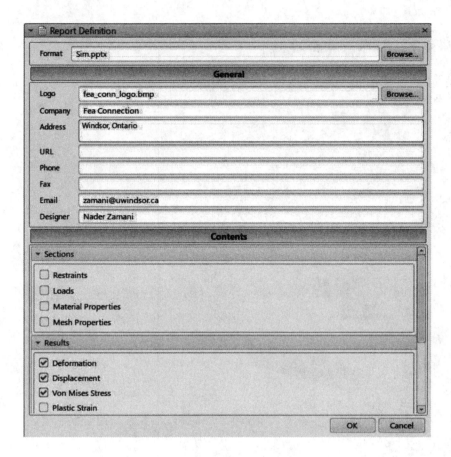

As a sample report, a very short one with three pages only, see the next page.

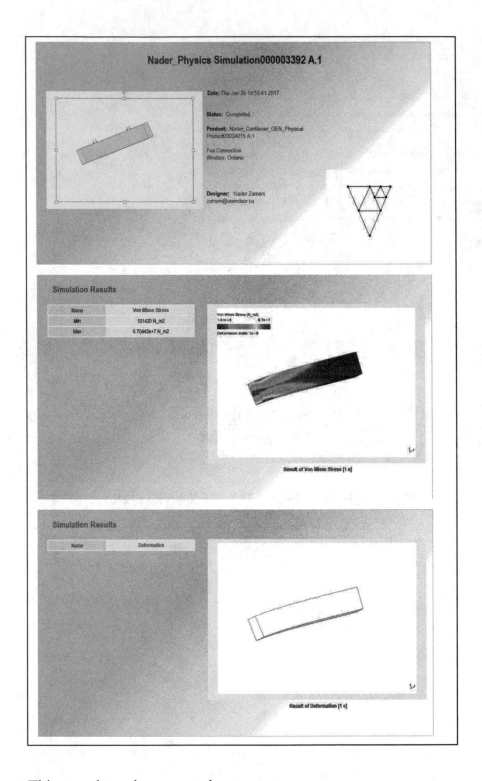

This completes the present chapter.

Exercises

Problem 1:

The foot pedal shown below is made of steel with Young's modulus 30E+6 psi and Poisson ratio 0.3. The pedal is loaded with a normal force of 100 lb along the edge shown. The other end of the pedal is clamped. The geometrical dimensions are provided at the bottom of the page where all the dimensions are in inches. Model the problem and predict the stresses.

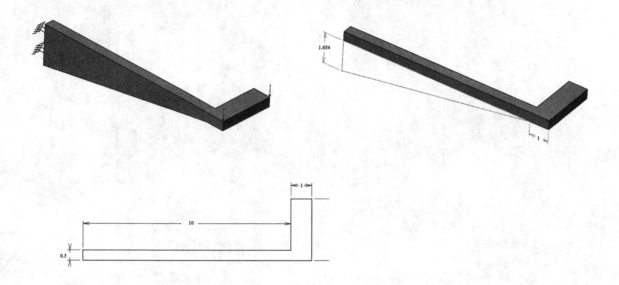

Problem 2:

The cylindrical bar shown below has a clamped end. The other end is subjected to a couple caused by opposite forces on magnitude 1000 lb separated by 1.5 in. This is equivalent to a torque of 1500 lb. applied to the cylinder. The material is steel with Young's modulus 30E+6 and Poisson ratio of 0.3.
The diameter of the cylinder is 1 in. and the dimensions of the loaded end are entirely up to you. Although not showing, the length of the padded cylinder is 5 in. and the length of the padded rectangle is 0.5 in. All sharp corners at the loaded end have surface fillet of radius 0.1 in. Model the part and predict the stresses in the part.

NOTES:

Scene Creation, Rendering, and Generating Video Clip

Objective:

This short chapter is designed to introduce some important functionalities which are hidden in the "Tools" tab of the action bar. These functionalities are scene creation and lighting, realistic rendering, screen capture, and video capture.

Creating a Model:

Using dimensions of your choice, create a part which is roughly what is shown below.

Looking at the action bar, there are two "arrows" shown there. The ones at the extreme left and right deal with navigating to the left and right. These two arrows allow you to get to the icons that cannot be seen due to the screen size and resolution. There is a different type of arrow ⊙ shown in the middle; this gives access to secondary menus that can be hidden.

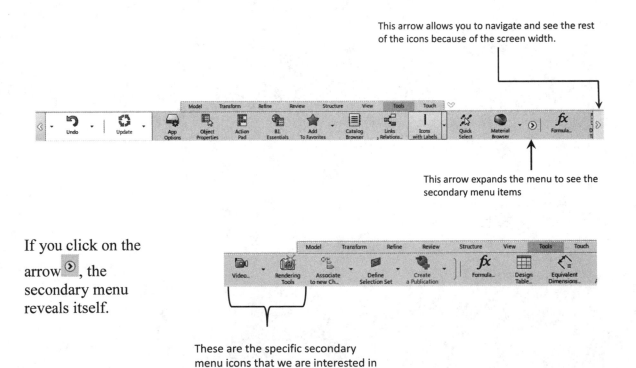

This arrow allows you to navigate and see the rest of the icons because of the screen width.

This arrow expands the menu to see the secondary menu items

If you click on the arrow ⊙, the secondary menu reveals itself.

These are the specific secondary menu icons that we are interested in

In this chapter, we will be discussing "Rendering Tools" 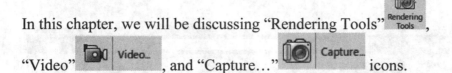,

"Video" 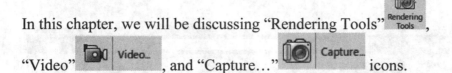, and "Capture…" icons.

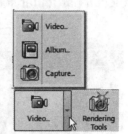

Select the "Rendering Tools" icon from the action bar.

The "Render" pop-up box appears. There are five options to choose from in this box, all listed in the figure on the right.

Choose the first button on the left side, named "Select

Scene" .

A database of the images (Scenes) available appears, shown below. This window has three tabs.

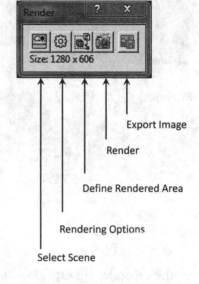

Export Image

Render

Define Rendered Area

Rendering Options

Select Scene

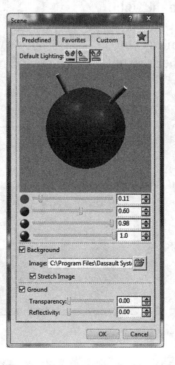
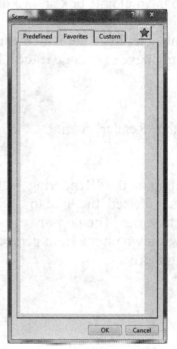

Select a particular scene from the database. This will place the scene behind your part.

Select the "Rendering Option" button 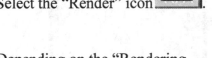. This leads to the dialogue box shown on the right.

Keep the defaults in the window unless you absolutely have to change it for other reasons.

Select the "Render" icon .

Depending on the "Rendering Options" selected, the time to complete varies. The pop-up window shown on the right persists during the process.

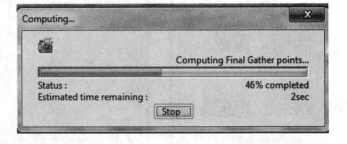

The rendered image is shown below.

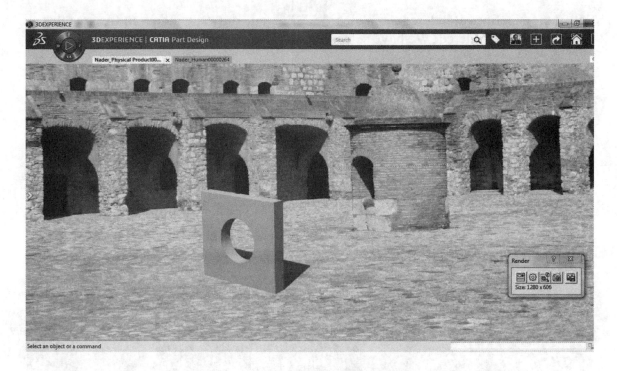

For your reference, the original image is also shown below. Note the lighting and the shading effect of the part (the geometry that you constructed) in the above image.

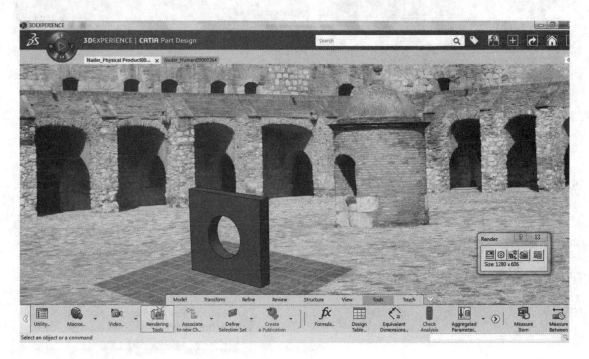

Select the "Defined Rendered Area" icon and draw a window in the area that you want to be rendered. We have selected the window below. Click on the "Render" icon .

This will render only a particular area and therefore, there may be considerable saving of the CPU time and computer resources.

Select the "Export Image" icon . This guides you to the directory in the computer to decide on the name and the image format. You can save render images.

The different available formats are shown on the right.

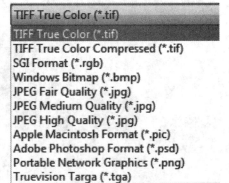

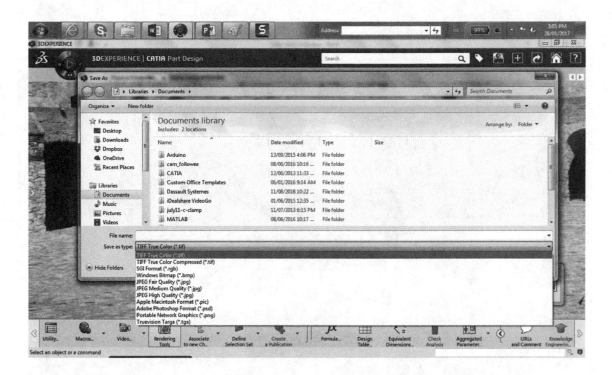

In the second tab of the "Scene" window you have the ability of selecting "no Lights" or "Two Lights" as shown below. You can also adjust the lighting source along some other parameters.

The rendered images on the next page were produced with "No Light" and "Two Lights."

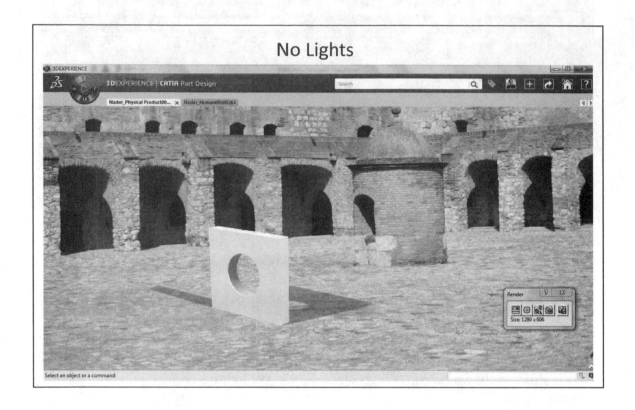

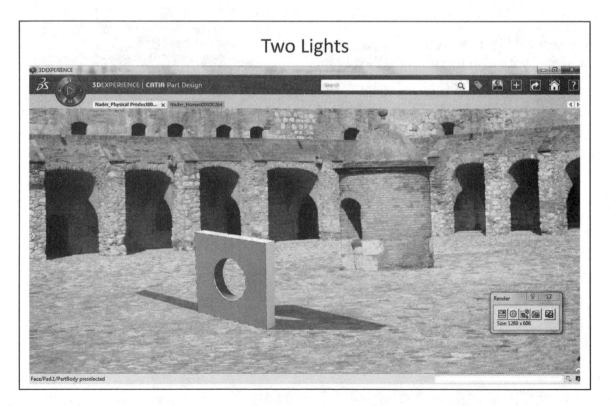

You can import your own image by going to the third tab of the "Scene" dialogue box. Select your desired image and check the "Stretching" box. After you close the window, click on the "Render" icon 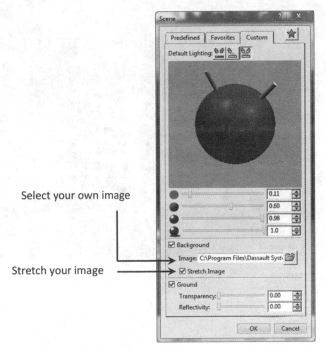 again. Your own image will be used for rendering purposes as shown below.

Select your own image

Stretch your image

Your own image here

Your own image

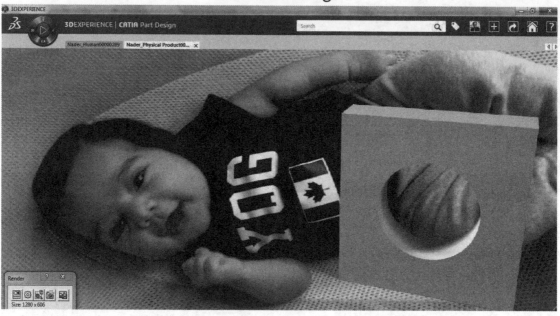

One can create an album which can be used for personal images. Click on the "Album"

icon 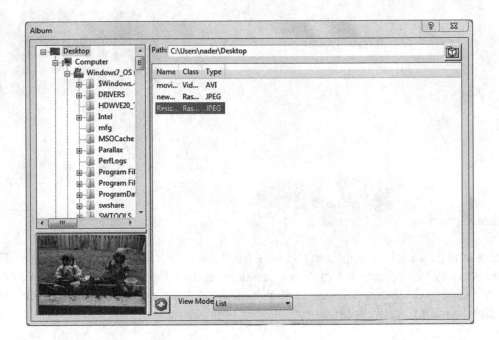. This will lead you to the folder where selections of your images can be made.

Capturing Images Utility 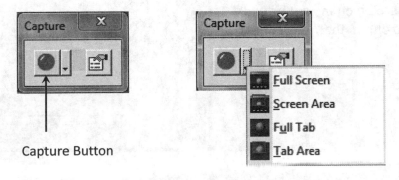 :

This is a very useful utility that allows one to capture images on the 3DEXPERIENCE screen. Click on the "Capture" icon.

This leads to the dialogue box shown on the right. Click on the "Capture" button.

Capture Button

Full Screen
Screen Area
Full Tab
Tab Area

The resulting captured screen shown below can be saved, printed and manipulated as desired.

Video Creation  :

This is a utility tool for capturing videos from the 3DEXPERIENCE sessions. The purpose may be creating tutorials, or capturing animations from mechanism motion, or finite element deflection modes. Selecting the "Video" icon leads to the following pop-up window which is self-explanatory.

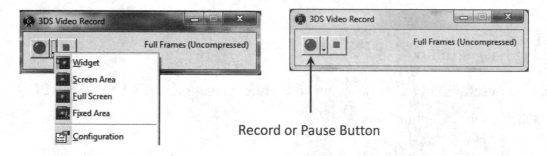

Record or Pause Button

Once the "Stop" button is pressed 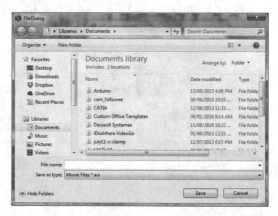, you are given the opportunity to save the video clip in the "avi" format.

Human Model (Manikin)

Objective:

CAD tools are primarily used to design components whose end users are human beings. The word "component" is used in a loose sense. For example, designing a workstation or an assembly line also qualifies for this definition. In such cases, human comfort (ergonomics) may be of major concern. In order to assess the quality and feasibility of such environments, human models (manikins) are used for simulation purposes. In this chapter, a quick tour of the functionalities in 3DEXPERIENCE for this purpose are presented.

There are mainly four Apps relevant to this subject in 3DEXPERIENCE. The Apps are listed below with icons also provided

1- Ergonomics Evaluation,
2- Ergonomics Manikin Editor,
3- Human Design,
4- Ergonomics for Car Design.

In the present chapter, the first three of these applications will be discussed by only scratching the surface of the available content.

Creating a Manikin  :

Click on the WEST sector of the compass on the top left corner of the screen. This will open the CAD applications available in 3DEXPERIENCE.

From the list, select the "Ergonomics Manikin Editor" Application.

The "Human" dialogue box shown on the right appears. You have the opportunity to modify the default name and make other selections with the available tabs.

Upon closing the dialogue box, the manikin appears on the screen.

The action bar (at the bottom of the screen) appears as shown below.

Note that for the created manikin, the gender can be changed.

Selecting the "Population" icon 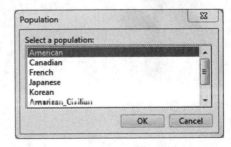 allows you to choose the nationality of the manikin from the resulting dialogue box.

Selecting the "Anthropometry" icon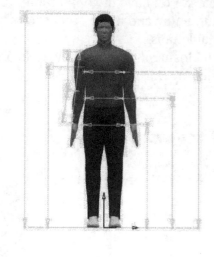
allows you to make certain changes in the
dimensions of the manikin.

While in this feature, click on the "Variable List"

icon ; you are presented with a list of
different dimensions that can be set. The List is
displayed below.

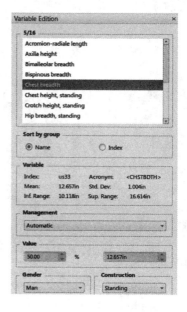

Changes can be made by selecting the "Manual"
option in the pulldown menu of the "Management"
section.

Close the "Variable Edition" dialogue box and select
the "Reach" icon. This will give you the dimensions
that cannot be observed in the front view.

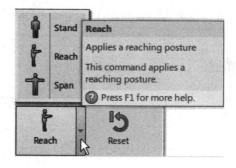

Click on  to exit "Anthropometry."
Select the "Product Edition" tab.

Product Edition

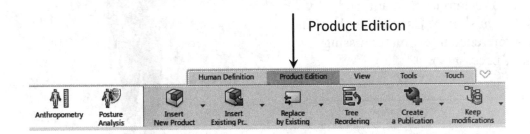

Now you will have the opportunity to create a CAD object. Select the "Insert New 3D Part" icon from the

menu [Insert New 3D Part].

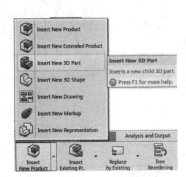

The pursuing dialogue box pertains to the 3D part to be constructed.

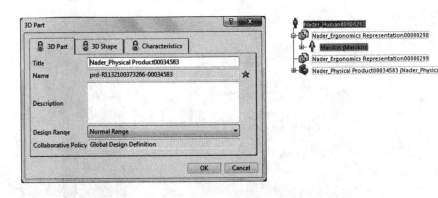

Double clicking on the "3D_Shape" branch of the tree will land you in the Part Design App. This is where a simple geometry will be created.

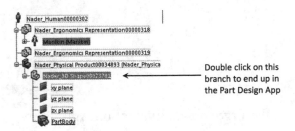

Double click on this branch to end up in the Part Design App

Choose the "Model" tab.

Select the xy-plane, and enter the sketcher. In the sketcher, draw a rectangle. Exit and pad it by roughly the height shown. Use the height of the manikin as a reference to estimate missing dimensions (if necessary).

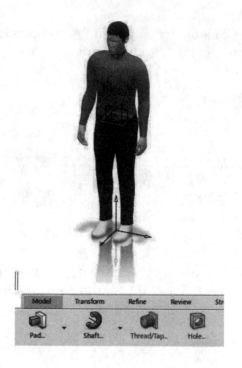

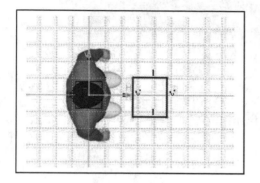

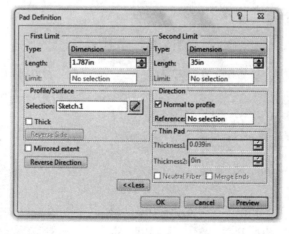

Using the South sector of the compass, select the Ergonomics Evaluation App from the list.

The action bar changes to what is shown below.

Select the "Reach Target" icon  from the action bar. Use the cursor to pick the corner of the block, followed by the manikin's left hand. Repeat the process for the right hand of the manikin. You will see that both hands are placed on the block.

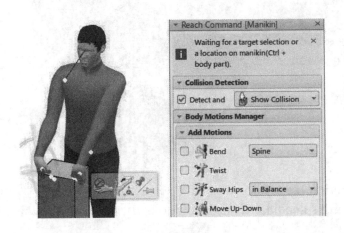

Select the "Joint Angle

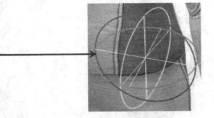

Manipulation" icon Angle Mani...; other configurations of the manikin can be obtained by manipulating the "Gyro."

Gyro For Joint Manipulations ⟶

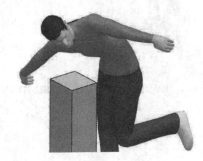

Select the "Posture" tab from the action bar.

Posture tab

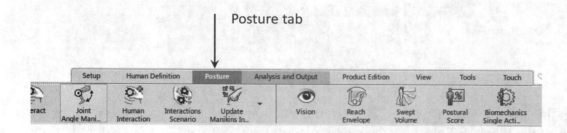

Choose the "Reach Envelope" icon from the list followed by the right hand of the manikin. The envelope of the possible movement of the hand is calculated and displayed.

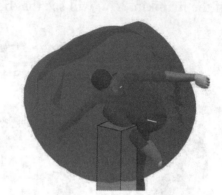

The rendering of different images of the manikin are in the "View" tab of the action bar.
Depending on the nature of the rendering selected, the manikin looks different as shown below.

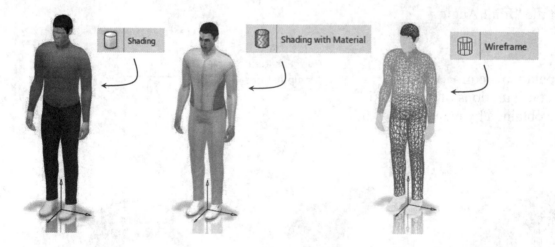

There have been substantial improvements in a more sophisticated application dealing

with human models. This can be found in the "Human Design" App .

Click on the WEST sector of the compass on the top left corner of the screen. This will open the CAD applications available in 3DEXPERIENCE.

From the list, select the "Human Design" Application 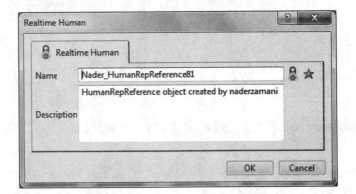.
You are prompted by the "Realtime Human" dialogue box. Press "OK."

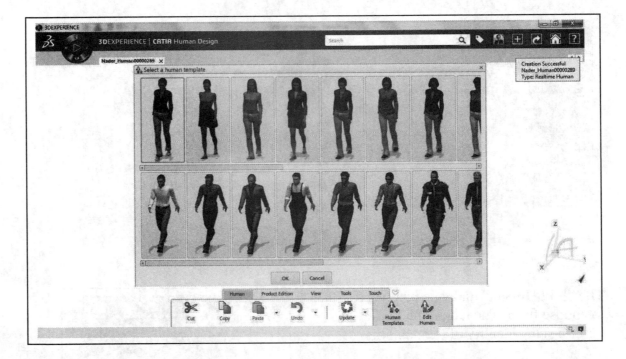

You are presented with a catalogue of manikins to choose from. We have selected the 4th one from the right on the top row. The screen changes appearance as shown on the next page.

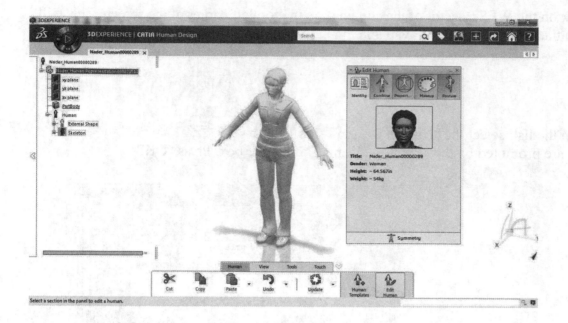

Change the rendering to "Material with Shading" to get the following configuration.

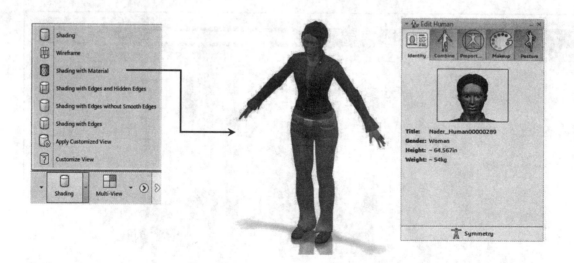

The "Edit Human" dialogue box has five tabs
to choose from. The tab on the far left
describes the identity of the manikin.

Select the "Posture" tab 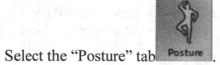.

The "Body posture preset" has many configurations to choose from, e.g., Standing, Sitting....

Four such configurations are selected and displayed below.

 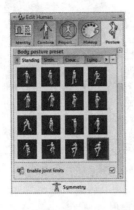

 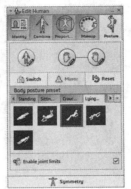

While in the "Posture" tab, select the "Finger Mode" and see the effect.

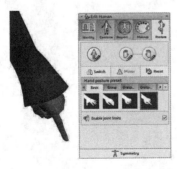

Select the "Makeup" tab, the second one from the right. This allows you to choose a variety of makeup as detailed as eyelashes.

Complexion/ facial powder

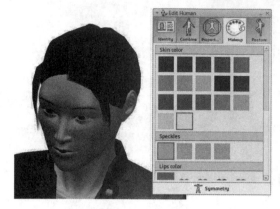
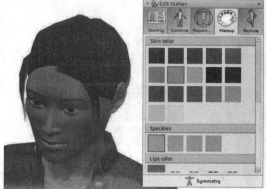

Eyelashes

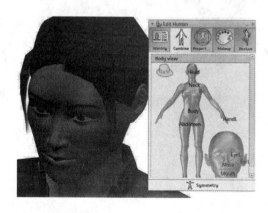
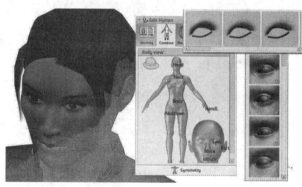

Select the "Proportions" icon 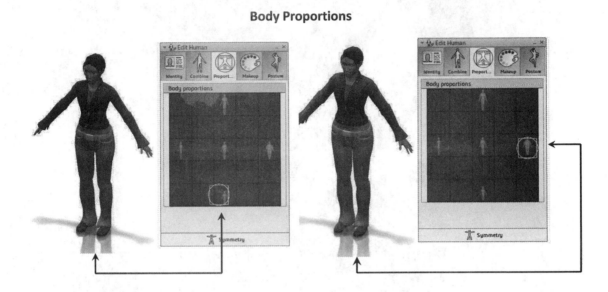, i.e., the middle tab. This describes the body proportions. Compare the two proportions selected from the menu.

Body Proportions

Select the "Posture" icon once again. You can drag the joints shown below to produce the configuration on the next page.

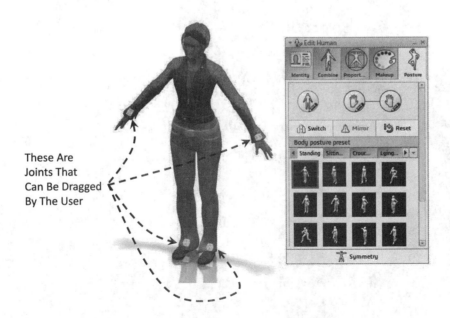

These Are
Joints That
Can Be Dragged
By The User

Select the "Combine" tab  and from the menu, choose the "Hat" . This allows you to select an outfit (among other things) for the manikin.

Select Outfit

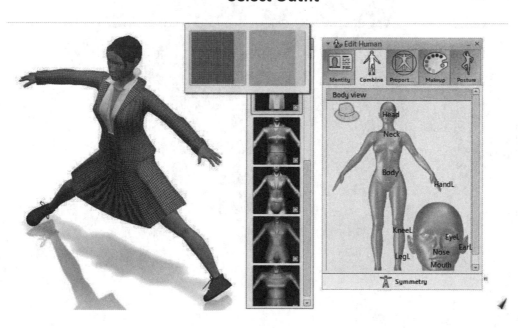

Double clicking on the manikin's hair allows you to
specify the hair style.

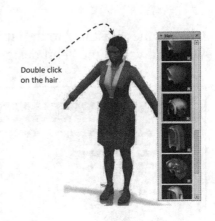

Double click
on the hair

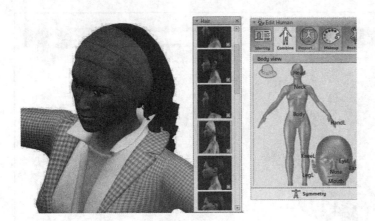

Using a Manikin to Create a Scene:

Human Design

Create the following manikin in the "Human Design" App .

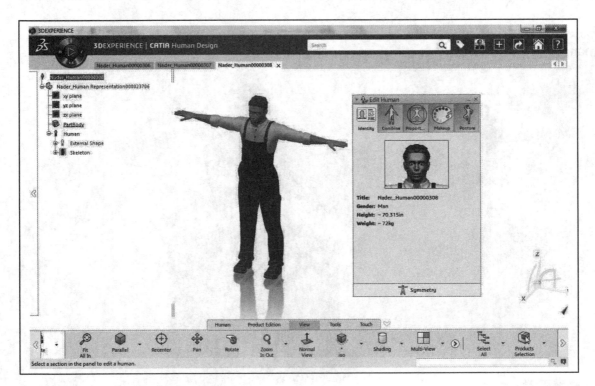

Change the "Posture" to the sitting position. Double click on "PartBody" in the tree. This will land you in the "Part design" App as shown below.

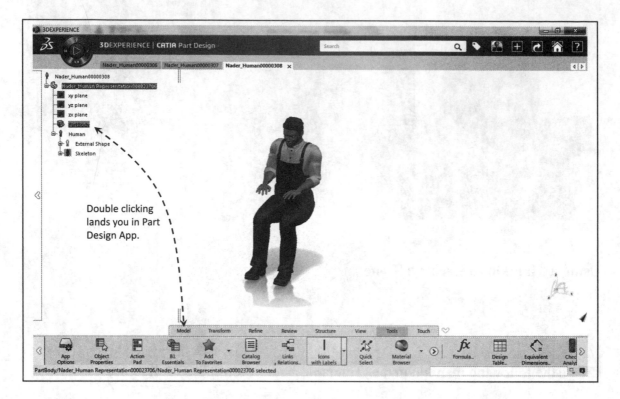

Enter the sketcher, and create a box in the position shown. If necessary translate the manikin (or the box).

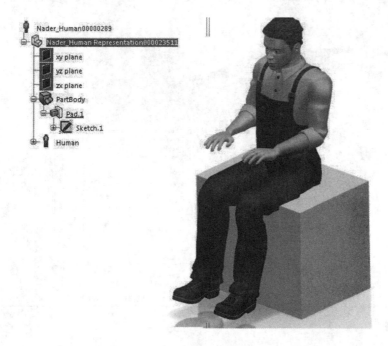

Use the process described in chapter 18 to create a "Scene."

Select the predefined image below from the database.

Select the "Render" button.

About Us

SDC Publications specializes in creating exceptional books that are designed to seamlessly integrate into courses or help the self learner master new skills. Our commitment to meeting our customer's needs and keeping our books priced affordably are just some of the reasons our books are being used by nearly 1,200 colleges and universities across the United States and Canada.

SDC Publications is a family owned and operated company that has been creating quality books since 1985. All of our books are proudly printed in the United States.

Our technology books are updated for every new software release so you are always up to date with the newest technology. Many of our books come with video enhancements to aid students and instructor resources to aid instructors.

Take a look at all the books we have to offer you by visiting SDCpublications.com.

NEVER STOP LEARNING

Keep Going

Take the skills you learned in this book to the next level or learn something brand new. SDC Publications offers books covering a wide range of topics designed for users of all levels and experience. As you continue to improve your skills, SDC Publications will be there to provide you the tools you need to keep learning. Visit SDCpublications.com to see all our most current books.

Why SDC Publications?

- Regular and timely updates
- Priced affordably
- Designed for users of all levels
- Written by professionals and educators
- We offer a variety of learning approaches

TOPICS
3D Animation
BIM
CAD
CAM
Engineering
Engineering Graphics
FEA / CAE
Interior Design
Programming

SOFTWARE
Adams
ANSYS
AutoCAD
AutoCAD Architecture
AutoCAD Civil 3D
Autodesk 3ds Max
Autodesk Inventor
Autodesk Maya
Autodesk Revit
CATIA
Creo Parametric
Creo Simulate
Draftsight
LabVIEW
MATLAB
NX
OnShape
SketchUp
SOLIDWORKS
SOLIDWORKS Simulation